THE BLOCKING OF ZEEBRUGGE

Operation *Z.O.* 1918

STEPHEN PRINCE

First published in Great Britain in 2010 by Osprey Publishing,
Midland House, West Way, Botley, Oxford, OX2 0PH, UK
44–02 23rd St, Suite 219, Long Island City, NY 11101, USA
E-mail: info@ospreypublishing.com

Print ISBN: 978 1 84603 453 4
PDF e-book ISBN: 978 1 84908 259 4

Page layout by: Bounford.com, Cambridge, UK
Index by Alan Thatcher
Typeset in Sabon
Maps by Bounford.com, Cambridge, UK
3D BEVs by Alina Illustrazioni
Originated by PPS Grasmere Ltd, Leeds, UK
Printed in China through Worldprint

10 11 12 13 14   10 9 8 7 6 5 4 3 2 1

A CIP catalogue record for this book is available from the British Library

THE WOODLAND TRUST

Osprey Publishing are supporting the Woodland Trust, the UK's leading
woodland conservation charity, by funding the dedication of trees.

EDITOR'S NOTE

All times given are Greenwich Mean Time (GMT) which corresponds to
the time used in British reports of operations. It should be noted that
German timings were actually recorded in documents in local Belgian
time, which was one hour ahead of GMT but they have been converted to
GMT in this account to avoid confusion.

The following abbreviations are used throughout the text:

CMB	coastal motor boats
DSO	Distinguished Service Order
ML	motor launch
RAF	Royal Air Force
RM	Royal Marines
RMA	Royal Marine Artillery
RMLI	Royal Marines Light Infantry
RN	Royal Navy
RNAS	Royal Navy Air Service
RND	Royal Naval Division
USN	United States Navy
VC	Victoria Cross

Illustrations are from the following sources, unless otherwise noted:

NHB	Naval Historical Branch
RNM	Royal Naval Museum
RMM	Royal Marines Museum

ACKNOWLEDGEMENTS

I would like to express my gratitude to Kate Moore and Philip Smith at
Osprey for their exceptional patience and great assistance to me. I would
also like to thank my colleagues at the Naval Historical Branch,
particularly Kate Brett, Jenny Wraight, Major Mark Bentinck and Captain
Chris Page RN and the staff of the National Museum of the Royal Navy.
Thanks go to Wing Commander Polly Perkins RAF, Commander Sean
Winkle RN and Olga Winkle. Amelia and Lucy Slay were of great help and
Lt Col Debbie Slay RAMC was inspirational. I would also like to dedicate
this book to my father and the memory of my mother.

FOR A CATALOGUE OF ALL BOOKS PUBLISHED BY OSPREY MILITARY
AND AVIATION PLEASE CONTACT:

Osprey Direct, c/o Random House Distribution Center,
400 Hahn Road, Westminster, MD 21157
E-mail: uscustomerservice@ospreypublishing.com

Osprey Direct, The Book Service Ltd, Distribution Centre,
Colchester Road, Frating Green, Colchester, Essex, CO7 7DW
E-mail: customerservice@ospreypublishing.com

www.ospreypublishing.com

CONTENTS

INTRODUCTION

Launched on St George's Day, 23 April 1918, the British raids on the Belgian ports of Zeebrugge and Ostend are among the most famous and controversial episodes of World War I. Sir Winston Churchill later wrote that they 'may well rank as the finest feat of arms in the Great War, and certainly as an episode unsurpassed in the history of the Royal Navy'.[1] More recent historians have been far less supportive, with one distinguished scholar stating that the raids 'won gallantry medals but no strategic advantage'.[2] The debate had begun even before the ships involved had returned to England and has continued ever since. All authors have acknowledged the great gallantry of the raiders, with a total of 11 Victoria Crosses being awarded across the three individual actions, but there has been no consensus on whether the operations led to any real military advantage for the Allies.

The raids were relatively simple in concept. Imperial German submarines, destroyers and torpedo boats were operating from the inland Belgian port of Bruges and by 1918 they were sinking around a quarter of all ships being lost off Britain. The distance of Bruges inland acted as an effective protection from Allied bombardment. The German vessels based there accessed the sea via a network of canals which connected to open water at the coastal ports of Zeebrugge and Ostend. The Royal

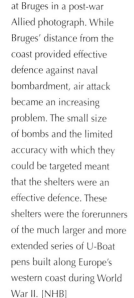

The German U-Boat shelters at Bruges in a post-war Allied photograph. While Bruges' distance from the coast provided effective defence against naval bombardment, air attack became an increasing problem. The small size of bombs and the limited accuracy with which they could be targeted meant that the shelters were an effective defence. These shelters were the forerunners of the much larger and more extended series of U-Boat pens built along Europe's western coast during World War II. [NHB]

1 Churchill, Sir Winston, *The World Crisis 1916–1918, Part II*, Thornton Butterworth (London, 1927) p.371.
2 Grove, Eric, *The Royal Navy Since 1815 A New Short History*, Palgrave (Basingstoke, 2005) p.139.

Sailors of the Royal Naval Division (RND) manning defences at Antwerp in 1914. The RND was an *ad hoc* formation, formed by Winston Churchill, using sailors for whom there was no immediate employment afloat. Initially the formation resembled a large scale landing party, as shown by the dated arms and equipment of these men. These formations had frequently been successful throughout the Royal Navy's history but World War I was a far more challenging conflict than those encountered in the decades before. The men had little infantry training and no supporting arms. They were intended to be used for landings, raids and port defence, but were rushed to help defend Antwerp in October. As it became clear the defence was not viable, the division retreated, losing over 2,400 men to capture or internment in Holland. [NHB]

Navy (RN) planned to seal these canals by sinking blockships at their entrances, thus trapping the German ships. At Zeebrugge, where the canal entrance was protected by a large projecting sea wall or 'Mole', it was also intended to place a converted cruiser alongside the Mole. This cruiser would then disembark a mixed force of Royal Marine (RM) and Royal Navy storming parties. The attack was designed to destroy German defences, or at least distract and occupy them, so that the blockships had a better chance of reaching their objective. The crews of the blockships were to be rescued by a supporting force of motor launches and destroyers, with monitors, cruisers and aircraft providing bombardment and cover for the assault force.

The German defences were formidable in number, sophistication and integration having been steadily developed during over three years of German occupation. At Ostend, the more limited of the canal exits, the defences completely frustrated both the initial raid and the attempted follow-up attack on 10 May. At Zeebrugge the raiders succeeded in putting the cruiser HMS *Vindictive* alongside the Mole to attack and distract the defenders and two of the three blockships were sunk in the canal entrance. Britain immediately claimed a significant success in blocking the canal and frustrating German sailings for weeks, with continuing disruption thereafter. By contrast Germany claimed that the British raiders had been defeated and, in the words of Admiral Scheer, commander of Germany's High Seas Fleet, 'that connection between the harbour at Zeebrugge and the shipyard at Bruges was never interrupted even for a day'.[3] The significance of the Zeebrugge raid, as for many prominent raids, has always been as much about its psychological impact and utility for propaganda, as about the direct physical effects achieved.

Reconciling these incredibly diverse views of the operation, with the literature often falling into overwhelmingly supportive or critical camps, is one of the main difficulties of assessing the raid. However, it is possible to achieve a balanced account. This involves examining the operation from both the Allied and the German side, the latter of which is often neglected but for which there are now also some excellent English language sources. It also involves placing the raid in the wider context of the campaign for access to the eastern end of the English Channel, a campaign that was crucial to the survival of the Entente powers (originally the British Empire, France and Russia) and one which was fought throughout the four years of World War I.

2–3 OCTOBER 1914

Mines laid north of Ostend.

---

3 Scheer, Reinhard, *Germany's High Sea Fleet in the World War*, Cassell & Company (London, 1920) p.339.

ORIGINS

Britain's concern about potentially hostile control of the north-west coast of Europe, particularly what is now the coast of Belgium and Holland, has endured for centuries. Naval forces operating from this coast have had the opportunity to block or disrupt Britain's vital maritime trade, exploiting the short ranges from this area to achieve rapid effects, often before superior Royal Navy forces could be deployed to intercept them. This concern has been one of the drivers for frequent British military involvements in the Low Countries, though ironically these involvements have then led to further concern about control of the coast because of the resulting army supply line. France's occupation of Belgium in 1793 was a *casus belli* for Britain's series of wars with France until 1815. Britain was then instrumental in ensuring that the 1837 Treaty of London established a Five Power guarantee of both Belgium's independence and its neutrality. When Britain declared war in August 1914 Germany's infringement of Belgian neutrality was the immediate cause. Not only did this attack challenge Britain's view of international law and behaviour, but its particular location meant it was also seen as a significant threat to Britain's survival.

This concern was also an accurate reflection of Germany's ambitions, with control of Belgium and later Holland, including their ports, remaining a German war aim throughout the conflict. Belgium's largest port, Antwerp, was captured in October 1914, despite an attempt by Winston Churchill, then First Lord of the Admiralty, to intervene with the Royal Naval Division (RND), at that point an *ad hoc* land force consisting of units of both Royal Marines and sailors. However, Antwerp's use as a naval base in a long war was frustrated by the fact it could only access the North Sea via the Scheldt Estuary, passing through the waters of neutral Holland. Germany assessed that such a violation of Dutch neutrality would result in British intervention against Holland, which would mean that Holland would not be available to Germany as an important trade partner, providing a route for indirect imports from other countries.

By mid-October, however, German forces had reached the Belgian seaboard, and by November they were in virtually full occupation of the coast, holding 30 miles of seaboard including Ostend and Zeebrugge. Both were minor ports compared to Antwerp but Zeebrugge in particular had enjoyed considerable investment and

The 'Mole' at Zeebrugge before World War I. It was constructed to provide Belgium with a major port that, unlike Antwerp, was not subject to access via Dutch waters. However, the structure also provided a ready-made fortress for the Germans, adjacent to sea lanes vital to British trade and to communications with the army in France. [NHB]

development before the outbreak of war. Belgium's ancient inland port of Bruges had lost its access to the sea centuries before due to estuary silting, but in the late 19th century plans were laid to renew its link to the sea via canals, thus giving Belgium a major port independent of Holland. In 1895 construction began on a 24ft-deep canal from Bruges to Zeebrugge. The development also included a massive sea wall, which would allow large ships to berth on its inner side. This curved sea wall, known as 'the Mole', had a length of nearly 1½ miles. The Mole included a section of lattice steel viaduct, close to the shore, which allowed the tidal current to continue to scour the inner side of the Mole, preventing it from silting up. The main section of the Mole was over a mile long and 80 yards wide and included a higher, reinforced wall on the outer side to protect against the elements. Depending on the state of the tide the top of this wall was 30–45ft above sea level but it also included an inner walkway 4ft below the parapet and about 16ft above the main surface of the Mole. At the seaward end of the Mole was a 15ft-wide extension which led to a lighthouse. The redevelopment was a commercial success, with the new port facilities opening for trade in 1905 and with over 800 ships using the port in the year before the war. However, what had been designed to withstand the demands of nature now provided a ready-made fortress for the German invaders.

The Belgian coast was placed under the command of Vice-Admiral Ludwig von Schroder and almost immediately his division was expanded to a corps, MarineKorps Flandern. This was one of the earliest examples of a unified, or joint, command, with Von Schroder commanding all sea, land and air forces on the Belgian coast in order to achieve a fully integrated defence of the base area. Von Schroder had joined the newly created Imperial German Navy in 1871 and early in his career served with the future Admiral Alfred von Tirpitz, who would become his most significant sponsor within the navy. After further service in operational units, both afloat and ashore, he moved to the Naval Staff in 1895 as Head of Section A3, responsible for planning mine and torpedo warfare. While in this post he completed a study of how Germany could exploit the Belgian coast in a war with Britain. In this study he particularly identified Zeebrugge and Ostend as potentially valuable advanced naval bases. In 1913 Von Schroder retired from the navy as head of the Baltic Naval Station, but on 24 August 1914 Von Tirpitz immediately recalled him to command the Belgian coast. His experience, studies and connections with Von Tirpitz made him a natural choice for the command and he would lead the MarineKorps Flandern until Germany evacuated the Belgian coast in October 1918.

This cross-section illustrates the construction of the Mole and its junction with the metal lattice section of viaduct, close to the shore. The lattice was essential to allow the sea to scour the Mole and prevent the harbour silting up. The diagram also shows the height of the Mole parapet above the water level. Even at high water there was still a difference of over 27ft. Finding a way to address this gap was fundamental to the success of any attack. [NHB]

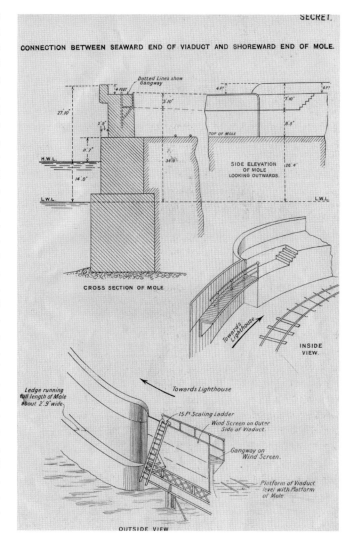

SECRET.

CONNECTION BETWEEN SEAWARD END OF VIADUCT AND SHOREWARD END OF MOLE.

CROSS SECTION OF MOLE

SIDE ELEVATION OF MOLE LOOKING OUTWARDS.

INSIDE VIEW

OUTSIDE VIEW

A UC I class submarine. This was a wartime class of 15 coastal minelaying submarines, the majority of which served in Flanders. They had a crew of 14, could lay 12 mines and had a range of 800–900 nautical miles, making forward basing essential for their operations. All were launched in 1915 but some survived as long as 1918 with UC.4 only being scuttled off the Flanders coast at the time of the German withdrawal in October 1918. [NHB]

By the end of 1914 four U-Boats were based at Zeebrugge, and on New Year's Eve 1914 one of them, U.24, torpedoed and sank the Channel Fleet's pre-dreadnought battleship, HMS *Formidable*, the first battleship ever to be sunk by a submarine. Reliance on inland facilities and the limitations of the ports and canals meant that only smaller coastal submarines and minor warships, up to destroyers, could be maintained in Flanders. This limitation, though, was partly mitigated by the fact that the bases were 400 miles closer to the ships' target waters off Britain than if they had been based in German ports. Such a location, only 70 nautical miles from the Thames Estuary, meant that some German coastal submarines could be used operationally against British merchant shipping when their range would have precluded any such role from German ports. This also permitted Germany to continue to maximize submarine numbers by investing in these relatively cheap and quickly constructed boats. By late 1916 there were 16 coastal submarines based in Flanders, including improved types which meant that the range and capacity per boat were also improving.[4] During 1916 these Flanders submarines found they were still able to pass through the Straits of Dover, avoiding the British defences which had proved more problematic for the larger submarines of Germany's High Seas Fleet. Indeed as a result of these defences, the High Seas Fleet U-Boats had suspended their use of this route in April 1915, with the effect that larger submarines had been forced to transit to their hunting areas off Britain or in the wider oceans via the north of the British Isles, thus adding approximately 1,400 miles to their passages and reducing their effective time on station, targeting shipping, by up to 40 per cent.

German torpedo boats passing through a lock at Ostend. Though there has been much attention paid to the submarine threat from the Flanders bases the Royal Navy was at least as concerned about German surface ships. Torpedo boats and destroyers had the potential to cause serious and rapid losses and disruption to the communications of the British Expeditionary Force (BEF) in France. [NHB]

---

4 For more details on the development of German submarines see Williamson, Gordon, *U-Boats of the Kaiser's Navy*, Osprey (Oxford, 2002).

German submarine activity up to this point had been frustrated, not just by the limitations of its own new technology and the extended passages required for larger boats, but also by the emphasis placed on the operations of Germany's main battle fleet, the High Seas Fleet. Germany's primary naval strategy was to use this fleet to confront Britain's Grand Fleet in the North Sea. However, as the High Seas Fleet was inferior to Britain's Grand Fleet in numbers this was only to be attempted under carefully controlled conditions, in order to try to achieve a favourable local balance of forces during the immediate action. U-Boats were a vital element in this strategy, both for reconnaissance and to ambush major British warships. Achieving these conditions proved to be very difficult, however, partly because the Grand Fleet operated cautiously in order to maintain its superiority and because Britain's advantages in signals intelligence often meant that the Royal Navy had foreknowledge of most German sorties. Even after the battle of Jutland on 31 May 1916, Admiral Scheer still sought to ambush the Grand Fleet using fleet sorties supported by submarines, but by October 1916 Germany's high command decided to resume submarine warfare against commerce. One result of this decision was that in the same month 24 destroyers were transferred from the High Seas Fleet to the MarineKorps Flandern.

The role for these ships, which would now reinforce Flanders periodically, was to counter British light forces in the Channel and facilitate access for the Flanders U-Boats through the Straits. Their tasking represented a new emphasis in German naval strategy, with the submarine becoming not just a weapon supporting the battle fleet but the main attacking force. The destroyers were required because the RN had begun laying large-scale minefields against the Flanders bases from April 1916 onwards. These consisted of both moored mine nets and barrages of deep mines and were initially laid off the Flanders coast. By September 1916 large-scale mine barrages were also being laid across the English Channel itself, broadly north-east of the vital Dover–Calais ferry route and south-west of a line from Harwich to Zeebrugge. On the night of 26/27 October German destroyers attacked the British barrages, sinking a destroyer, a transport and six drifters before escaping unharmed. The raid illustrated the vulnerability of the British defences and led to more RN destroyers being moved into the area, even though this limited the ability of the battleships of the Grand Fleet

17 OCTOBER–7 NOVEMBER 1914

Bombardment of Belgian coast.

31 DECEMBER 1914

Zeebrugge-based U.24 sinks HMS *Formidable*.

The Mole showing a submarine shelter constructed on the inner side of the wall to protect against air and naval bombardment. These shelters were adequate for brief periods but having ships and submarines alongside the Mole for long periods was too dangerous and so German units were actually based inland. While this reduced their vulnerability it also affected their operational performance. The canals took several hours to navigate and the RNAS, and later the RAF, undertook extensive reconnaissance, meaning that ships were often spotted in transit to the sea. [NHB]

to operate with proper screening forces. On both sides the demands of directly attacking or protecting commerce were assuming a higher priority, relative to fleet operations.

The German destroyers were able to continue periodic raids, with some tactical successes, through the winter of 1916–17. However, they were only able to operate as 'guerrilla' fighters in the Channel, attacking only under the cover of darkness; this gave them something of a 'seasonal' element, which relied on long winter nights. They had to retreat before more powerful RN forces could reach them and were unable to fundamentally disrupt the vital flows of either general trade or cross-Channel transports for the British Army, as there were often 50 ships at sea each night. Despite being only a little over two hours' steaming away they were frustrated by both the size and exposure of the Belgian ports. This meant that destroyers were the largest warships that could operate so close to British communications and even these ships had to move inland to avoid British naval and air bombardments. This limited their flexibility to operate quickly, particularly given regular British air reconnaissance to determine their movements through the canals. However, their operations did help to determine the relative ineffectiveness of the British minefields at this point and so encouraged continued transits by Flanders submarines through the Channel, providing a short route to the shipping beyond. From January to November 1917 it is believed that only one U-Boat was lost to a Channel minefield, even though U-Boats made over 250 Channel transits.

The German destroyers were also instrumental in preventing the RN from maintaining the coastal minefields offshore from Ostend and Zeebrugge, a barrage codenamed 'Zareba' after the African term for a thorn bush hedge used against predators. Five thousand 'Zareba' mines were laid in April–May 1916. The barrage was initially successful, resulting in the sinking of three U-Boats (UB.13 on 24 April 1916, UC.3 on 27 May 1916 and UC.7 on 5 July 1916), but the presence of the destroyers, German naval aircraft and an increasing number of powerful coastal guns, with calibres of up to 38cm, meant it was not viable in the longer term. Britain's counters to the Flanders forces were effectively restricted to the use of very long-range artillery, firing both from ashore and from monitors in the Channel, supplemented by air attacks. This bombardment forced the Germans to divert some of their offensive effort and invest in a wide range of defences, including their own mines, coastal patrols by ships and aircraft and extensive passive shelters for facilities, ships and personnel at all their Flanders bases. However the bombardment had very little destructive effect. The very range which protected the British and French gunners also militated against the accuracy required to hit targets which were both small and invisible to them. While aircraft had more potential, particularly against Bruges, and were important for reconnaissance, their load capacity and accuracy were still too immature to have a significant effect and they were frequently diverted to higher priority tasks in support of the British Expeditionary Force (BEF). Therefore by late

UB.23, a Type UBII class submarine, many of which served in Flanders. UB23 was commissioned on 13 March 1916 and served in Flanders. The submarine had a crew of 23 and a range of around 6,500 nautical miles on the surface, a huge improvement over earlier UB types with ranges of less than 2,000 nautical miles. This greatly increased the effective threat posed by the submarines' armament of two torpedo tubes and a 5cm deck gun. UB.23 was interned at La Coruna, Spain, after being damaged by the RN patrol boat P 60 and surrendering to France in February 1919. [NHB]

A 12in Mark X naval gun is landed at Dunkirk from the deck of the monitor *General Crauford* on 5 April 1916. The gun weighed 58 tons and so had to be carefully rolled ashore using tractors and 5½in wire parbuckles. These weapons were mounted in the sand dunes of Dunkirk and manned by the Royal Marine Artillery. Admiral Bacon had requested them to bombard Ostend and as counter-battery weapons against the increasing number and size of German guns on the Flanders coast. Seven of these guns were cycled through Dunkirk between 1916 and 1918. [NHB]

1916 there was an element of balance and mutual frustration in the Channel. The RN was successfully maintaining communications with France, and the German surface ships from Flanders could gain tactical victories but not severely disrupt British operations. However, the RN had yet to find any effective measure to counter the Flanders U-Boats transiting the Channel and accessing the open sea via the short route, with the MarineKorps Flandern's integrated defence system preventing sustained close mining or bombardment.

The impact of the Flanders boats was at first limited, as was that of all German submarines, by self-imposed restrictions on their operations. They were generally not permitted to sink merchant ships without warning, a practice known as 'unrestricted warfare' which greatly improved their effectiveness when it was allowed. The limitations were self imposed rather than voluntary because they resulted largely from American diplomatic pressure on Germany. Germany's leadership initially calculated that the limitations on its submarines were more than offset by keeping America out of the war. This caused Germany twice to draw back from unrestricted submarine warfare in 1915 and 1916. By the start of 1917, however, under the strain and apparent stalemate of the war, Germany's leaders amended their position and committed to unrestricted submarine warfare, which commenced on 1 February 1917. The German estimate was that with just over 100 U-Boats available, 23 of them based in Flanders, and by operating unrestricted submarine warfare they would be able to sink 600,000 tons of merchant shipping a month. It was assessed that the losses would also terrorize at least 40 per cent of neutral merchant shipping into abandoning their transport of cargoes to Britain. The end result of these physical and psychological losses would be unbearable to Britain after about five months and Britain would have to sue for peace. Within that timescale the risk of American intervention in the war could be tolerated as America would not be able to mobilize in time to make a significant impact.[5]

The German campaign met with spectacular initial success, with sinkings rising from 369,000 tons in January to 881,000 tons in April, the month that the USA declared war on Germany. Sinkings remained high, with 597,000 tons lost in May and 688,000 tons in June, but were now in overall decline and would never again reach

---

5 For the best full discussion of these issues see Halpern, Paul, *A Naval History of World War I*, UCL Press (London, 1994), particularly Ch.11.

A 28cm gun, one of four, of the Tirpitz Battery, sited two miles west of Ostend. Installed in 1916, Tirpitz was one of the earlier heavy batteries of the MarineKorps Flandern. Though sited near Ostend its long range of 32,000m (35,000 yards) meant it was able to engage targets along most of the coast, including off Zeebrugge or behind the Entente lines near the coast. The Germans built up a sophisticated system of combined land, air and sea defences, weapons and sensors that was a precursor of current policies of 'network-centric' warfare. During the retreat from Belgium in 1918, the facilities were extensively demolished to prevent the system from being analyzed. In a pre-radar era the great limitation of the system was in accurately responding during limited visibility, though this was normally also a problem for attackers. The raids of 1918 sought to exploit the visibility issue to the full, relying on accurate navigation and route marking during their attacks. [NHB]

April's figure. The reasons behind this were complex and included a series of ruthless measures by Britain to ensure that neutral ships did not cease trading with Britain, to increase the productivity of shipping and to limit consumption through rationing. The most important single factor, however, was the increasingly widespread introduction of convoys. Convoys had been implemented for troopships from the outbreak of the war and had progressively expanded for high-value cargoes thereafter. The Admiralty was at first reluctant to implement them more widely, both because of legitimate reservations about their disadvantages, such as port congestion and ships being delayed by slower vessels, and because of misperceptions about merchant trade, such as the assumption that more ships were engaged on oceanic routes than was actually the case. By May the convoy system, with essential support from the United States Navy (USN), particularly over the provision of escorts, was spreading and had the effect of emptying the seas of targets for the U-Boats. In addition Britain's advantages in radio intelligence meant convoys could often also be routed away from submarines. When the U-Boats did find convoys they also found they were now subject to counter-attack by the RN and USN, as well as aircraft.

Nevertheless, losses still remained serious, ranging between 250,000 and over 500,000 tons of shipping from July 1917 to October 1918, only then going into sharp decline as Germany was in final retreat.[6] Losses continued to outstrip new merchant ship building, which was limited by increased naval building requirements, until the second quarter of 1918. This was of particular concern given the requirement to find the shipping capacity to deliver a vast new American army to France in 1918 and 1919. Therefore though the anti-submarine issue had been apparently controlled it remained a serious threat for the rest of the war, with a constant awareness that a new German tactic or technology could once again dramatically increase results. One of the ways Germany did maintain its tonnage total was by moving the focus of its attacks away from the open oceans to the coastal areas around Britain, where there were far more shipping movements and well-protected convoys were less likely to be encountered. While there was a series of local counter-measures such as coastal convoys and increased air observation these took time to become effective. In this new campaign the smaller Flanders U-Boats, able to make the short Channel passage to these coastal hunting areas and then spend long periods on patrol, were being disproportionately effective and so the focus on these boats and their bases, and finding any effective means to counter them, was renewed.

6 Tonnage losses are taken from Fayle, C.E., *Seaborne Trade, Volume III*, John Murray (London, 1924) p.465. They have been rounded to the nearest 1,000 tons and are inclusive figures for all causes, but submarines are the overwhelming cause, particularly from 1917 onwards.

INITIAL STRATEGY

Britain's initial offensive against the Belgian ports was undertaken as early as the night of 2/3 October 1914 when four cruisers laid mines just north of Ostend, as a result of the German advance through Belgium. Ironically, within 36 hours it became necessary for the RN to sweep a channel through its own minefield as plans changed and British land forces were landed through Zeebrugge to try to support Belgium! (In a further irony two of the four minelaying cruisers, HMS *Intrepid* and HMS *Iphigenia*, would return to Zeebrugge in 1918 as blockships.) By 12 October this attempt had been abandoned and both Zeebrugge and Ostend evacuated. However, the ports had not been sabotaged, largely because of the widespread assumption of a fairly short and mobile war and the resulting expectation that the ports would soon be back in friendly hands and required for the landing of army supplies. The RN felt unable to dispute the resulting army request to leave the ports intact but the potentially serious threat from even temporary German occupation of the ports was recognized. On 13 October the Dover Strait was removed from the control of the Admiral of Patrols. A new command, the Dover Patrol, was established, initially commanded by Rear Admiral the Honourable Horace Hood. This command, including ships, guns ashore and, from 1915, aircraft of the Royal Naval Air Service (RNAS), was the direct counterpart to MarineKorps Flandern and would remain so for the rest of the war.

Though the Dover Patrol's fundamental task was to keep coastal waters open for merchant shipping it was initially concerned with direct support to the land battle, seeking to prevent further German advances down the coast towards the French Channel ports that the British Expeditionary Force (BEF) relied on for its communications. From 17 October to 7 November 1914 an Anglo-French squadron carried out bombardments along the Belgian coast between Nieuport, which marked

LATE 1915

Rear Admiral Bacon proposes Ostend landing.

The area of operations of the Dover Patrol 1914–1918.

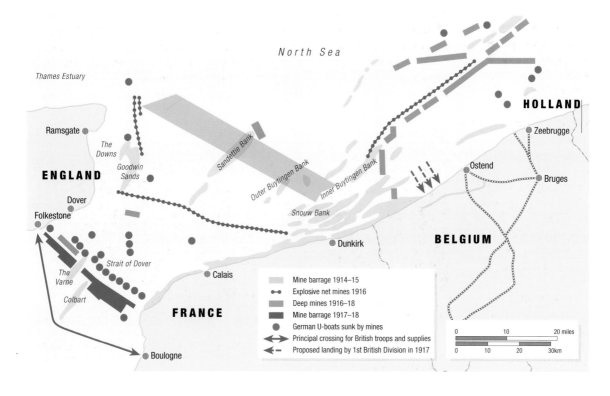

Legend:
- Mine barrage 1914–15
- Explosive net mines 1916
- Deep mines 1916–18
- Mine barrage 1917–18
- German U-boats sunk by mines
- Principal crossing for British troops and supplies
- Proposed landing by 1st British Division in 1917

13

the end of the Entente-held coastline and was held by the Belgian Army, and German-occupied Ostend. Partly as a result of this naval fire Nieuport was held and the German advance arrested. Interestingly, the bombarding ships in these operations included the cruisers HMS *Brilliant* and HMS *Sirius*, ships that would later be used as the blockships at Ostend. By the end of the period, however, the first German heavy guns were appearing on the coast and the dangers of coastal bombardment were becoming apparent; the destroyer HMS *Falcon* was hit by a German shell, losing nine killed, including her captain, and 14 wounded. While the Dover Patrol continued to carry out coastal bombardments to support the ground forces Rear Admiral Hood was increasingly convinced they had little value unless they were coordinated with offensive action ashore.

Such offensive action, with the particular objective of Zeebrugge, was discussed almost as soon as the port was in German hands. Admiral Jellicoe, commander of the Grand Fleet, consulted with Admiral Bayly, commanding the Channel Fleet, in late 1914. They considered the use of blockships against the canal entrance but the Admiralty considered the concept impractical. The perceived impracticalities included the ability of the enemy to repair any damaged facilities while the Germans still occupied the coast. The Admiralty's reaction may also have been linked to wider possibilities that Churchill was already pressing for, which addressed that objection. Churchill proposed a large-scale flanking attack along the coast, with Zeebrugge as the target. On 22 November he wrote to Sir John French, Commander-in-Chief of the BEF:

> If you chose to push your left flank along the sand dunes of the shore to Ostend and Zeebrugge, we could give you 100 or 200 heavy guns in absolutely devastating support. For four or five miles inshore we could make you perfectly safe and superior. Here at last you will have your flank – if you care to use it: and surely the coast strip held and fed well with troops would clear the whole line out almost to Dixmude and hand it right back, if it did not clear it altogether. If the attack was quick and sudden, their big guns would all be caught too. We could bring men in at Ostend and Zeebrugge to reinforce you in a hard south-eastern push. There is no limit to what could be done by the extreme left handed push and sea operation along the Dutch frontier.

Churchill's proposal demonstrated the first suggestion of a considerable naval operation against the Belgian ports, though in this case a major landing, coordinated with a ground offensive. He also later wrote to French, 'Zeebrugge, I feel sure ... at the critical moment – and as the theory of your attack – can be assailed from the sea; and then kick back to Ostend.'[7] Lord Kitchener, the Secretary of State for War, attempted to limit the army's involvement and proposed a mainly naval operation. Lord Fisher, the First Sea Lord, was prepared to consider a landing of thousands of troops at Zeebrugge but still only in conjunction with an army advance. All of these plans also required the British Army to occupy the coastal section of the western front, which was currently held by the Belgian Army. When General Joffre, the French Commander-in-Chief on the western front, refused to consider such a reallocation of frontage, which might have interfered with his offensive plan, the concept of a joint attack was postponed in January 1915. Resources were then concentrated on other operations on the western front and naval forces in particular were diverted to the prospective campaign at Gallipoli, with Churchill now giving this operation a higher priority.[8]

---

7 Sir Winston Churchill to Sir John French, 22 November 1914 and 1 January 1915, both quoted in Wiest, Andrew, *Passchendaele and the Royal Navy*, Greenwood Press (London, 1995) pp.8 and 19.
8 See Haythornthwaite, Philip, *Gallipoli Frontal Assault on Turkey*, Osprey (Oxford, 1990).

On 13 April 1915 Rear Admiral Hood was succeeded by Rear Admiral Sir Reginald Bacon. Admiral Bacon had served in the RN from 1877 to 1909, including service in a 'naval brigade', a force of sailors and marines assembled to fight with the army ashore in Benin in West Africa in 1897, service for which he was appointed to the Distinguished Service Order (DSO). However for much of his career he been concerned with technology and ordnance and after retiring from the RN he had been managing director of the Coventry Ordnance Works. In 1914 he had gone to France as a colonel in the Royal Marine Artillery (RMA) commanding heavy howitzers ashore until Winston Churchill appointed him to the Dover Patrol.

Given his background, and the recent rejection of major action on the ground, it was unsurprising that Bacon concentrated much of his energy on trying to improve the effect of bombardment. He developed new spotting methods, involving placing tripod masts on the seabed, and methods for the recently available 12in gun monitors to fire while underway, thus reducing their vulnerability. On 23 August 1915 these new methods were applied against Zeebrugge, with the principal targets being the canal locks; further bombardments in September included Ostend. The results of the bombardments were ultimately disappointing, owing to the distances involved and the very small size of the vital targets. Also the presence of the 'Tirpitz' Battery of 28cm guns near Ostend, which now outranged the larger but older guns of the British monitors, demonstrated the increasing danger of German counter-battery fire. Bacon continued to try to develop the potential of bombardment, including mounting large naval guns ashore, to target facilities in the closer port of Ostend. However, like Hood before him, he was increasingly convinced that bombardment alone was not enough.

In late 1915 Bacon sent a memorandum to both the Admiralty and the BEF proposing a landing at Ostend. Earlier in the year Bacon had worked on a plan to actually block Ostend and Zeebrugge, in order to disrupt the minelaying work of the German submarines based there, which was then considered their most dangerous activity. This plan envisaged the use of blockships, bombardment and even a possible assault on the Mole, all elements of the plan ultimately enacted in 1918. Training was undertaken with the cruiser *Apollo*, which it was envisaged would have

Royal Naval Division wounded on the western front in 1918. After Antwerp the division served at Gallipoli and on the western front 1916–18. It gradually altered its composition to become a fully established division including army units, being formally renamed the 63rd (Royal Naval) Division and 'looking' more like a normal division, as illustrated in this photograph. It also became one of the elite divisions of the BEF. Over 8,000 sailors and marines died while serving in the division and another 20,000 were wounded. On four occasions the sailors and marines of the division took higher casualties in a single day than the raiders suffered at Zeebrugge. [NHB]

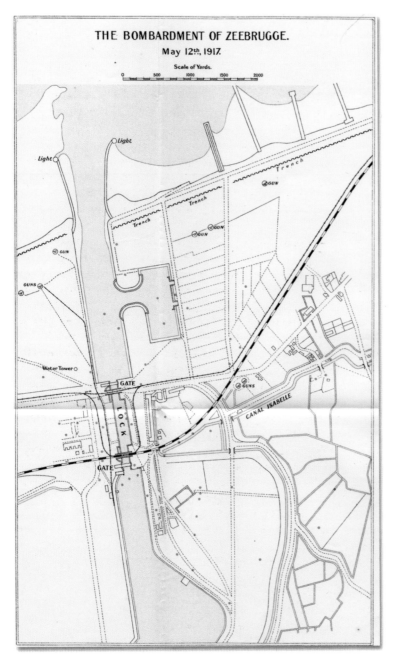

THE BOMBARDMENT OF ZEEBRUGGE.

May 12th, 1917.

Scale of Yards.

blockships lashed to it in order to deliver them into the canal. However the technical difficulties of achieving this were partnered with continuing Admiralty scepticism about the long-term effects of blockships when isolated from other offensive measures. Eventually the plan was shelved, as a new concept of assault emerged involving a landing at Ostend that would now require the port facilities in working order to support it. Bacon's later concept called for a large-scale landing based on a fleet of 100 trawlers and six monitors that he assessed could reach Ostend without serious loss. This force would then link with land forces which would have previously launched a large-scale offensive from both Nieuport and Ypres in the direction of Ostend. The attack was required both to occupy German reserves before a landing and to link up with the otherwise isolated landing force once the port had been seized.

The BEF's Commander-in-Chief, now Sir Douglas Haig, was sympathetic to the concept but was clearly concerned that some of Bacon's assessments were actually optimistic assumptions. He appointed General Sir Aylmer Hunter-Weston, who had recently commanded a corps at Gallipoli, to liaise with Bacon and consider the plan in detail. Hunter-Weston was more sceptical than Bacon, particularly over the likely losses to German coastal artillery, but ultimately the requirement to link the landing to a major offensive in the coastal sector meant it was again deferred. To achieve this would require Anglo-French agreement on its priority and this was not possible in 1916 against the evolving background of the battles of Verdun and the Somme. Bacon, though, continued to press for a landing, stressing the significance of retaking the Belgian coast, both for its impact on current operations and as an insurance against the development of future threats. For him this encompassed not just an increase in the threat from German units in the Belgian ports in the current conflict but also the possibility that Germany might be able to retain the Belgian coast in any compromise peace agreement, if it was still in occupation. If that were to happen then Bacon assessed that Holland, surrounded by German-controlled territory, would eventually come under

German domination and Britain's strategic nightmare of hostile domination of the whole of the north-west European shore would have been fulfilled.

Bacon also saw the opportunity to attack the Belgian coast as a declining possibility, due to the increasing density and range of German defences. In the spring of 1916 the 'Kaiser Wilhelm' Battery of 30.5cm guns with a range of 34,000 yards had become operational near Zeebrugge. From the summer of 1916, therefore, Bacon estimated that only landings on the less defended open beaches either east or west of Ostend would be feasible. The continuing problem, though, was that any landing, and particularly an advance near the Belgian ports, would need to conform to the larger pattern of the war ashore. This seemed unlikely in 1916, especially once the battle of the Somme had commenced on 1 July, but continuing army interest in the concept is indicated by the fact that on 18 September Haig suggested to Bacon that tanks should be included in any landing, only three days after their first ever operational use in a land battle.

Several factors then coincided to make the prospect of a major landing, which became subsequently known as 'the Great Landing', more likely in 1917. First the German destroyer raids from 26/27 October 1916 onwards made the RN increasingly conscious of the potential level of threat against the Channel and the Thames Estuary from the reinforced forces in the Belgian ports. This anxiety was further heightened by the advent of unrestricted submarine warfare, with its accompanying great increase in losses, from February 1917. Jellicoe, now First Sea Lord, strongly advocated action against the ports, both because of the damage of submarines to trade and because he was apprehensive about the ability of the growing number of Belgian-based surface ships to disrupt cross-Channel communications with the BEF. Equally, he was clear that naval action alone could not neutralize the ports, and that only occupation of the Belgian coast would fundamentally deal with the threat. Jellicoe's position reinforced General Haig's preference for a major British offensive from Ypres. Haig proposed that when this offensive reached Roulers conditions would be right for a further subsidiary offensive at corps level along the coast from Nieuport, which would also be combined with a divisional level landing between the German front line and Ostend. Some historians assert that Jellicoe's support was critical to Haig's gaining permission to launch his offensive, while others have argued, more convincingly, that Jellicoe's role was far less significant, particularly given that the use of convoys was starting to control shipping losses by the summer of 1917.

Whatever the balance of factors behind the decision for the third battle of Ypres, very serious preparations were made for both the coastal advance and the landing. From May onwards Bacon and Sir Henry Rawlinson, commander of 4th Army, the army that would be responsible for both the offensive by XV Corps from Nieuport and the amphibious landing, were in regular contact. The planned landing was to be west of Ostend and on a divisional scale, with a landing force of around 14,000–15,000 troops. Bacon had already proposed that they be delivered by very large shallow-draft pontoons, each of which would be 540ft long and 30ft wide. Each of these 2,500-ton ships was to lift an entire brigade of infantry, including artillery and tanks. Each of the three un-powered pontoons was be pushed by a pair of 12in gun monitors, with trials confirming the feasibility of the system. Extensive use was made of aerial photographs to calculate beach gradients and training was then undertaken on similar beaches in Britain. Supports were engineered that would allow the nine tanks involved to cross the sea wall. The landing would also be shrouded by a smoke screen from 80 motor launches in an attempt to frustrate the German coastal artillery. In addition to these maritime preparations an entire division of troops, the 1st Division, was committed to intensive and secret training for the operation from July onwards. This realistic training steadily

OPPOSITE

The spread of hits (indicted by the red dots) of the Royal Navy's bombardment of Zeebrugge, 12 May 1917. The bombardments continued through the war but required particular and fairly rare combinations of tide and weather to make them feasible. The May bombardment involved 41 vessels, including four 12in and 15in monitors, one of which was *Terror*. Smokescreens from motor launches were used to limit the visibility of the German batteries and 250 heavy shells were fired against the lock. Though several rounds came close, none struck the gates and no substantive damage was caused. The frustrating limits of isolated, long-range bombardment were again illustrated, providing further evidence for the requirement for a landing or raid. [NHB]

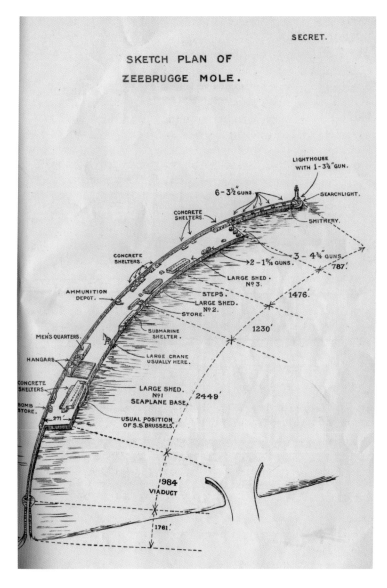

SECRET.

SKETCH PLAN OF
ZEEBRUGGE MOLE.

LIGHTHOUSE
WITH 1 - 3½" GUN.

6 - 3½" GUNS

SEARCHLIGHT.

CONCRETE
SHELTERS.

SMITHERY.

CONCRETE
SHELTERS

3 - 4¾" GUNS.
2 - 1¾₆" GUNS.
787'

LARGE SHED.
Nº 3.

AMMUNITION
DEPOT.

STEPS.
LARGE SHED.
Nº 2.
STORE.

1476'

SUBMARINE
SHELTER.

1230'

MEN'S QUARTERS.

LARGE CRANE
USUALLY HERE.

HANGARS.

CONCRETE
SHELTERS

LARGE SHED.
Nº I
SEAPLANE BASE.

2449'

BOMB
STORE.

271'

USUAL POSITION
OF S.S. BRUSSELS.

984'
VIADUCT

1761'

A sketch of the Mole in 1918, showing the FlandernMarine Korps' developments. Basing facilities had been added for submarines and aircraft, with the shelter of the Mole being particularly useful for launching seaplanes. [NHB]

increased the ability of the veteran troops, with one of the soldiers recording that:

... we were introduced to the greatest secret of all in connection with our camp. This was an exact replica of the sea-wall at Ostend, the same steep, wet, slippery concrete, the same greasy sea-weed hanging to it; a really marvellous piece of work ... At first glance, yes even after our first try, we thought the feat of surmounting the slippery wall was impossible ... But inch by inch as it were, we mastered the sea wall of Ostend ... In time we were masters, and were able to carry up all sorts of things, Lewis-guns, reels of telephone wire, bundles of barbed wire, in short, anything that would be necessary in the real thing in Ostend.[9]

After a successful landing and linkup it was planned that Ostend, if not captured, would now be within range of field calibre artillery, the massed fire of which would soon render it untenable. Zeebrugge would not be subject to this intensity of fire but Bacon was confident he could bring several of the new 18in naval guns ashore, behind the new and closer front line and that these would also be able to disable the canal lock.

German awareness of the increased possibility of attack, particularly along the coast, had, however, manifested itself even before training had begun. On 10 July 1917 the MarineKorps Flandern attacked the small British bridgehead north of the River Yser, adjacent to the coast. This intensive offensive destroyed the two British infantry battalions present, both of them from 1st Division. Though the battalions could be reconstituted, the attack meant that the Germans now held one side of the river as a natural and stronger defensive line in the coastal sector. The 'Great Landing', though, was ultimately frustrated not by this local setback but by the much larger-scale failure of the Ypres offensive, which would become known as the third battle of Ypres or Passchendaele. From the first attack on 31 July progress was behind schedule, with the result that the coastal offensive and the landing were continually postponed.

This delay led to the frustration that was such a common experience for the commanders planning action against the Belgian ports. On 22 August 1917 General

9 Jackson, John, *Private 12768 Memoir of A Tommy*, Tempus (Stroud, 2004) pp.136–37.

18

Rawlinson wrote a memo urging that the landing should go ahead in September not because the pre-requisite advances had been made but because they had not been made and he thought that the landing might provide an important diversion. Haig's headquarters rejected this not just because of the likely scale of losses that would result from an isolated landing but also because it was thought that a failed landing would be used by Lloyd George's government to further challenge Haig's authority and divert troops away from France. No landing at all was therefore favoured unless there was a high chance of success. As the main fighting inland never came close to generating this chance the operation was finally cancelled on 15 October 1917, though some contingencies were left in place to allow an attempt to remount it in 1918. The intensively trained 1st Division was released to a conventional role in the fighting.

How feasible the landing would have been must remain speculative, especially in view of how dependent it would have been on the larger military situation whenever it was launched. Most of the commanders directly involved were optimistic about the prospects for success given the short distance behind German lines that the amphibious hook was targeted on and the high standard of training of the assault division. However, analysis including the German sources is more pessimistic. In particular the extent to which the German coastal artillery could be rendered ineffective by smoke for an extended period of time was very doubtful and the MarineKorps Flandern had nearly twice as many troops available to counter-attack the landing as the British forces had allowed for, unless they had already been drawn off by serious fighting elsewhere. The balance of evidence suggests that the 'Great Landing' would have been unlikely to succeed unless it had been firmly placed in a pattern of much wider advances.

Whatever the reasons, the cancellation was a bitter disappointment for Bacon and meant that, despite the enduring losses and risk, no offensive had been launched to combat the threat from the Belgian ports except long-range bombardment and distant mining. At this point a new officer became involved in the campaign against the bases. He would be the driving force in planning and executing a new series of measures by the Dover Patrol, of which the raids on Zeebrugge and Ostend would be the centrepieces. He was Rear Admiral Roger Keyes.

The German gun battery on the Mole extension in a photograph taken after the German evacuation, with the guns having been disabled. These guns were thought to be 3.5in (88mm) weapons but were actually 4.1in (105mm) guns. They caused great damage to *Vindictive* during her final approach to the Mole, inflicting heavy casualties on the upper decks. However the successful deception plans and smokescreens meant that *Vindictive* was only exposed for a short period and no fundamental damage was done to the ship. The action on the Mole also meant these guns inflicted no damage to the approaching blockships. [NHB]

THE PLAN

OPPOSITE

Vice-Admiral Roger Keyes, commanding the Dover Patrol in 1918. A distinguished sailor before this command, Keyes was a firm believer in the need for offensive action, many would say even to the point of recklessness. He launched the raids on Zeebrugge and Ostend as part of a wider pattern of operations in the English Channel designed to achieve both physical and psychological dominance over German forces. Had the Germans coordinated naval attacks with their land offensives of 1918, there could have been very serious consequences. Such coordination was ultimately unlikely due to Germany's internal tensions but Keyes' operations helped reinforce a defensive mindset amongst the German forces in Flanders. Keyes was created KCB immediately after the raids and went on to be commander-in-chief in the Mediterranean (1925–28), a Conservative MP (1934–43) and a liaison officer to Belgium (1940). From 1940 to 1941 he was Director of Combined Operations until, frustrated by lack of activity, he resigned and was replaced by Lord Mountbatten. In this post, however, he laid the groundwork for successful combined operations later in the war, drawing on his pioneering experience from the raids of 1918. [NHB]

Roger Keyes was a cadet at the Royal Naval College, Dartmouth from 1885 to 1887 before serving at sea, including working in small boats against slavers and in a naval brigade in Witu, East Africa in 1890. He later commanded the destroyers *Hart* and *Fame* on the China Station and in 1900 led a cutting-out party that captured four Chinese destroyers during the Boxer Rising. Later he was part of the relief force that relieved the besieged international legations in Peking (Beijing). He ended that campaign with a reputation for initiative and daring in the eyes of some but for recklessness to others. What he did secure was a special promotion to commander. Keyes went on to serve in Naval Intelligence, to command a cruiser and to be commodore of the infant Submarine Service, the post he held when war broke out. Lord Fisher, the new First Sea Lord, was unimpressed with his record but Keyes' friendship with Winston Churchill assisted him and he was posted as Chief of Staff to Vice-Admiral Carden in the Mediterranean. Keyes served in this role under Carden's successor De Roebeck throughout the Gallipoli campaign, constantly urging offensive action, even in disagreement with his commander. He also became closely associated with another of the Gallipoli commanders, Admiral Rosslyn Wemyss. Appointed to command a Grand Fleet battleship in June 1916, Keyes was then promoted to rear admiral, second in command of the 4th Battle Squadron. This was a brief appointment as Wemyss was now Deputy First Sea Lord and arranged for Keyes to be appointed Director of Plans at the Admiralty from September 1917.

Keyes' main task was to develop counters to the use of the Straits by German submarines and to find a way to frustrate the Flanders bases. By the summer of 1917 a broad consensus had emerged between the Admiralty and Bacon that the existing mine and net barriers across the Channel must be improved. A new barrier, largely of deep mines laid at varied depths, was to extend across the Channel from Cape Gris-Nez to Folkstone, being commenced in November as sufficient quantities of more reliable mines became available. However there remained many differences between Bacon and the Admiralty over the tactics and emphasis that should be employed regarding the barrage. On 13 November Admiral Jellicoe appointed Keyes to chair a Channel Barrage Committee to consider the issues. Keyes' committee was uncompromising over its condemnation of current arrangements, reporting:

> That the complete ineffectiveness against submarines of the present barrier between Dover and Dunkirk is amply proved by the records from the NID [Naval Intelligence Division], which show that at least 253 passages have been made by enemy submarines through the Dover Straits, in 1917.[10]

While generally agreeing with the extensions to mining then being enacted the committee also stressed the requirement to provide the maximum and earliest possible illumination of the barrier at night, in order to try to force U-Boats down into the new minefields. This would require a large number of ships and patrol craft with searchlights and flares. Bacon objected to this, stating that the ships providing illumination would be vulnerable and proposing fixed lights on either side of the Channel supplemented by three or four special ships, 'bulged' against torpedo attack and equipped with lights and guns, ships that he was currently developing. Keyes

---

10 Keyes to the Secretary of the Admiralty, 29 November 1917, reproduced in Halpern, Paul, *The Keyes Papers, Volume I, 1914–1918,* Naval Records Society (London, 1972) p.419.

strongly disagreed with this gradual approach, stating that Bacon over-estimated the danger to illuminating ships, and supporting his argument for more urgent action with extensive intelligence about successful U-Boat passages. The issue came to a head in mid-December when Bacon was given a direct order by Jellicoe to institute a barrier patrol with maximum illumination as soon as possible. This first occurred on 19–20 December and that night UB.56 was lost to a mine when it dived to avoid the lights. This dramatic evidence was one of the catalysts for major changes in the Royal Navy's higher command. The First Lord, Sir Eric Geddes, decided to replace Jellicoe as First Sea Lord with his deputy, Sir Rosslyn Wemyss. Wemyss in turn sacked Bacon and replaced him with Keyes, who took up his appointment as commander of the Dover Patrol and an acting vice-admiral on 1 January 1918. Keyes was now in the rare position of being a military officer able to implement the policies he had planned and advocated.

Keyes immediately put maximum effort into the new barrage, rapidly assembling 70 craft to illuminate it at night. The results were gradual rather than spectacular with six U-Boats being destroyed between his appointment and the Zeebrugge raid but this contrasted with a maximum of only two destroyed before December 1917. The vulnerability of the patrol craft was, however, also illustrated when German destroyers raided the barrier on the night of 14–15 February 1918, their first raid since April 1917. Seven destroyers sortied from Germany, rather than Zeebrugge, though they refuelled there after the action. This was done to maximize surprise and was successful. The Germans sank six craft and damaged another seven, retiring without loss though one destroyer was damaged by a mine as it withdrew. Keyes was furious and instituted a series of disciplinary proceedings against local commanders and improvements to the tactical arrangements in the Channel. Moreover he considered that, while risking the patrol craft was essential and acceptable to prevent U-Boat movements, this also had to be part of a package of wider measures. In early December he had written to Admiral Beatty, now commanding the Grand Fleet:

> We will make Dover Straits unhealthy for submarines ... It will take time to do thoroughly and in the meantime I want to block Ostend and Zeebrugge. It can be done. Salvage people say the possibility of removing blockships quickly – the excuse given always – is much exaggerated – and in the mean time 25% of our losses continue to be caused by Flanders submarines, to say nothing of the nasty threat of a large destroyer flotilla on the flank of our communications.
>
> I pointed out in my recommendation that we shan't be asking the personnel engaged to take any more risk than the infantry and tanks take every time they advance to attack – and hundreds of officers and men would give anything to take part in such an enterprise.[11]

---

11 Keyes to Beatty, 5 December 1917, *ibid.* pp.422–24.

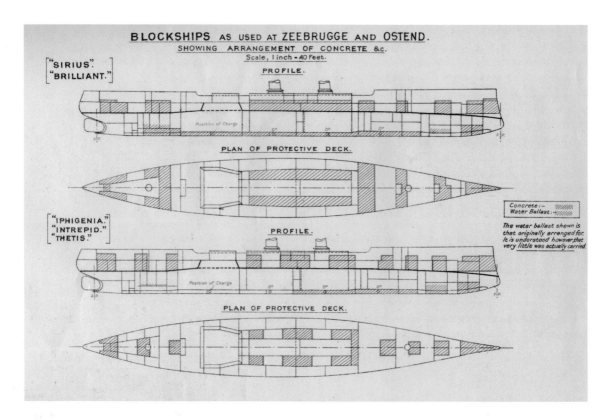

BLOCKSHIPS AS USED AT ZEEBRUGGE AND OSTEND.
SHOWING ARRANGEMENT OF CONCRETE &c.
Scale, 1 inch = 40 Feet.

"SIRIUS".
"BRILLIANT."

PROFILE.

PLAN OF PROTECTIVE DECK.

"IPHIGENIA."
"INTREPID."
"THETIS."

PROFILE.

Concrete :—
Water Ballast :—

The water ballast shewn is
that originally arranged for.
It is understood however, that
very little was actually carried.

PLAN OF PROTECTIVE DECK.

The conversion of light cruisers into effective blockships. This diagram illustrates the 1,000 tons of concrete introduced to each ship to increase the difficulties of salvage and the charges placed low in the hull to blow out the bottom of the ship. [NHB]

These themes, of integrating raids into the wider campaign of the Dover Patrol, equating the risks with those regularly taken by land forces and stressing the potential to link the raid with widespread frustration but also enthusiasm throughout the navy, were to be constants in his justification and planning of the raids.

While Keyes brought new commitment to planning the raids, he was also able to draw on the series of previous concepts for such an operation. In late 1916 and early 1917 Commodore Tyrwhitt had proposed a series of plans to attack Zeebrugge with a blockship, covered by bombardment, smoke and poisoned gas attack. He had then developed this theme to include an assault on the Mole, as a first stage to occupying Zeebrugge itself and developing a campaign against Antwerp. Keyes was well aware that this was far too ambitious for any resources likely to be available but was attracted by the blockship ideas that had been put forward by both Tyrwhitt and Bacon. He had the issue of salvage studied and interviewed Belgian refugee dock workers from Zeebrugge. He assessed that the constant silting of the harbours would make German salvage work to remove the blockships difficult, especially if the blockships had been heavily ballasted with concrete. He also proposed amending Bacon's earlier idea of delivering the blockships lashed to a cruiser to a concept of using old cruisers, which would approach under their own power, as the blockships. This was the basis for an initial plan which he submitted to Admiral Jellicoe while Keyes was still Director of Plans, on 3 December 1917, envisaging an assault in March 1918. Keyes addressed the possible objections of the army by stressing that the military situation made any advance up the coast unlikely for many months; he also made the point that the Germans were bound to block the ports themselves before abandoning them. Moreover he continued to equate the risks of the operation with the fighting ashore and suggested how naval enthusiasm could be harnessed while minimizing the security risks involved in a widespread recruitment:

At first sight, the blocking operations may be regarded, particularly at Zeebrugge, as a hazardous enterprise: but I feel very strongly that we shall not be asking the personnel engaged to take any greater risks, than the infantry and tank personnel are subject to, on every occasion on which an attack is delivered on shore.

A call for volunteers for such an operation would produce hundreds of officers and men. The necessity for secrecy would not permit this, but there should be no difficulty in selecting suitable officers, who similarly would be able to select men eager to take part in such an enterprise.[12]

A copy of the plan was accidentally sent to Bacon who suggested amendments, including adding an assault on the Mole, in the manner suggested by Tyrwhitt but without the ambitious follow-up into the town. He suggested that the assault force be delivered by the monitor *Sir John Moore*, which would approach the Mole bow on and secure a 12ft-wide brow, or landing platform, against it, over which 1,000 assault troops would pass. Bacon also planned that, under the cover of this assault, another monitor, *General Crauford*, would proceed inshore of the Mole and bombard the lock gate with 12in shells before the blockships attacked. The Admiralty approved this plan as a basis for preparations and with Bacon in command. In late December Keyes visited the Grand Fleet and gained Beatty's enthusiastic endorsement for raising volunteers from his ships, as well as submitting to the Admiralty a list of old cruisers which should be prepared for the operation.

Within days, however, Bacon had been removed and Keyes was now charged with commanding as well as preparing the raids. He considered the details of the attack during January and continued to amend the plan, even as initial preparations and training were undertaken. He rejected the idea of a monitor firing close inshore, seeing the blockships as the key weapon. As a result of this, he accepted Bacon's concept of the requirement to attack the Mole, in order to increase the chances of the blockships making a successful passage all the way to the canal, but rejected the idea that attack should come from a monitor. The ship's speed would have been reduced to only 4 knots by the false brow required to disembark the assault force and he felt this would be insufficient to cope with the current at Zeebrugge. He also considered that a single brow was too vulnerable as a point of failure, should it be struck by a shell before the landing force was on the Mole. He therefore looked to replace the monitor with multiple vessels and access ramps. He also adapted a further idea from Tyrwhitt's earlier plans to use extensive smoke screens in order to try to protect the entire force as it passed through the zone subject to German bombardment.

Keyes' final plan, the culmination of so many concepts and plans since 1914, was submitted to the Admiralty as 'Operation *Z.O.*' on 24 February 1918. Its major points were:

1. *Our Object*
To deny the use of Zeebrugge and Ostende to the enemy as bases for submarine and torpedo craft.

2. *Enemy vessels using the ports*
According to the latest information ... there are 38 submarines and 28 T[orpedo] B[oat]s (and T[orpedo] B[oat] D[estroyer]s) based at these ports. Submarines and destroyers can

SEPTEMBER 1917

Keyes appointed Director of Plans at the Admiralty.

3 DECEMBER 1917

Keyes proposes initial plan for March 1918 blockship attack on Zeebrugge.

24 FEBRUARY 1918

Final Operation *Z.O.* plan submitted to the Admiralty.

---

12 Reproduced in Keyes, Roger, *The Naval Memoirs of Admiral of the Fleet Sir Roger Keyes*, Thornton Butterworth (London, 1935) pp.132–33.

pass between Ostende and Zeebrugge and vice versa, by way of the canals via Bruges ... It is therefore necessary to block both ports.

According to the latest information in possession of the NID, the submarines operating from these ports are responsible for 25–30 percent of the number of merchant vessels sunk ...

Thus the use of several units would be lost to the enemy *so long* as the harbours remained closed.

There are about 30 destroyers based on Zeebrugge which are a continual menace to shipping in the Downs [the sea area off Dover] and to allied patrol craft. The removal of such a menace would release many of our destroyers at Dover for taking a more active part in anti-submarine work.

3. *Remarks on Blocking Zeebrugge*
...

The complete blocking of Zeebrugge ... entails block-ships being sunk in the entrance to the Zeebrugge–Brugges canal, i.e. within the extremities of the estacades (wooden piers) built out from the shore. At the shore end of the estacades the navigable channel narrows to a width of approximately 250 feet.

One block-ship of 250–300 feet in length might be sufficient, *but it is considered advisable to sink three block-ships so as to render success more certain.* ...

It is proposed that the leading blocker shall ram the outer lock gate and sink herself in the lock entrance. If this is successfully carried out it will be impossible for the enemy to use the lock until the obstacle has been removed. ...

The other two blockers should be sunk athwart the narrowest part of the navigable channel in such a manner as to overlap each other.

The plan detailed the five cruisers that had been assigned the role of blockships, three for Zeebrugge and two for Ostend, again to provide an overlapping barrier and increase the chance of success. It went on to suggest that salvage of the blockships would be particularly difficult, given the careful ballasting of the ships with large amounts of concrete, and estimating that cutting away the upper works of the ships 'would take months rather than weeks, during which time the channel would be silting up'.

The plan then went on to discuss the conditions of weather and visibility that would be required. These included a high tide to allow ships to assault the Mole parapet and an approach during darkness: 'a moonless night is considered preferable'. Wind coming generally from the north 'would be suitable for the use of smoke screens to cover the approach of the forces'. However wind coming generally from the south 'would be disadvantageous if its strength exceeded that of light airs'.

The plan also proposed a series of diversionary measures, both before and during the raid, aimed at 'diverting the enemy's attention from the true nature of the attack'. These included selective mining, in the hope that this would suggest to the Germans that there was little prospect of a British surface attack, as well as ship and air bombardments. These would target German patrol craft but:

Coastal motor boats (CMBs) were one of the workhorses of the Dover Patrol. The initial boats ordered in January 1916 were 40ft long, with 55ft versions being ordered from mid-1916. They could be equipped with a wide range of weapons, including 18in torpedoes and machine guns, had crews of two to five and some, with the most powerful engines, could achieve speeds of up to 42 knots. In the raids they were used mainly for smokelaying and rescue work. [NHB]

Another effect of such bombardments will be that of deceiving the enemy as to the true nature of the enterprise when the main operation takes place, the latter being prefaced by similar bombardments carried out from the sea and air.

Aircraft were also to be used on the night of the assault for 'illuminating the harbour entrances by means of parachute flares'.

The plan then went on to outline the concept that had been decided upon for the attack on the Mole:

14. *Attack on the Zeebrugge Mole by storming parties*

Near the northern extremity of Zeebrugge mole certain guns have been located. It is considered that these guns form a serious obstacle to the safe passage of our block-ships which will have to pass within one cable [approximately 200 yards] of these guns.

The batteries are believed to consist of 3–4.1[in] guns firing to the eastward, i.e. parallel to the line of the mole, and 4 or 5 smaller anti-aircraft guns whose arc of training is uncertain.

It is therefore very desirable to obtain temporary possession of the northern part of the mole before the block-ships meet with any opposition therefrom.

...

It is proposed to storm the mole from the seaward side, utilising [the cruiser] *Vindictive* and two ferry steamers from Liverpool.

...

The boat deck of *Vindictive* will be about 7 feet below the top of the parapet at high water.

The ferry steamers will require special ladders for disembarking troops, the length of the ladders being about 22 feet.

Vindictive is being fitted with flammenwerfers [flame throwers] and machine guns placed at such heights as to direct their fire on the mole in the nature of a barrage. By this means it is hoped that serious opposition to the landing will be swept away.

Vindictive is being fitted with one 11 inch and one 7.5 inch howitzer and a number of Stokes guns [mortars]. The howitzers are intended for engaging the more distant targets, such as the shore batteries, the lock, and the seaplane base at the western end of the mole. The Stokes guns are intended for use against the nearer works and the personnel on the mole.

Vindictive will also have guns of the main armament each side of the ship and is being provided with special anchors for securing to the parapet on arrival alongside.

...

Vindictive will be secured alongside the northern part of the mole about 300 yards from its extremity, i.e. abreast the mole batteries.

One Ferry Steamer will be secured alongside the mole ahead of *Vindictive*, the other Ferry Steamer will secure alongside *Vindictive*.

In the above positions none of these three boarding vessels can be hit by the shore batteries.

As soon as opposition has been cleared by means of flammenwerfers, machine guns, and hand grenades, the latter thrown over the parapet from the ship, the storming parties will storm the mole and set up their own barrage along it by means of Lewis and machine guns, rifle fire and hand grenades.

The first and main objective of the storming parties are the 4.1 inch guns which will be attacked in the rear and any enemy vessels which may be secured to the inner side of the mole, i.e. all war material which may otherwise be utilised against the block-ships.

Having carried out their main objects the storming parties will endeavour to destroy the remaining works on the mole.

The Seamen storming parties will divide into 4 units, each unit consisting of 2 officers and 50 seamen. Two of these units will go in *Vindictive* and one in each ferry steamer.

Each of the three boarding vessels will also take one marine unit consisting of 8 officers and 200 men.

The seaman units will be trained in securing the ship alongside the mole, in working the disembarkation ladders, in the use of Stokes guns and in demolition work.

The RMA personnel are being trained in the use of flammenwerfers, machine guns, and howitzers.

The R[oyal] M[arine] L[ight] I[nfantry] personnel are being trained in the use of Lewis guns, machine guns, hand grenades, bayonets, and in all types of night fighting at close quarters with the enemy.

The plan then outlined the intention to destroy the viaduct section of the Mole in order to prevent German reinforcements from reaching the fighting. In the plan it was envisaged that this would be achieved by exploding coastal motor boats (CMBs) but this was one of the few areas to be altered for the actual raid, with submarines taking the role. The role that remained for the CMBs, and most of the other vessels, was deploying the extensive smokescreen, described as 'being in the nature of a sea mist' that was considered vital to mask the ships from German coastal guns but which made the operation so wind dependent.

The earliest dates proposed for the operation, based on moon and tide, were 14–19 March, with a second window of opportunity on 12–16 April. For their approach on such dark nights it was stated that the block and boarding ships would be aided in their navigation by parachute flares from aircraft, as well as flare buoys laid by motor launches (MLs), fixes taken on the monitors providing supporting fire and searchlights from *Vindictive*.

Keyes recorded that the plan was returned to him around 4 March with comments from the Sea Lords. These comments were overwhelmingly supportive, with getting *Vindictive* into the right position being noted as one of the most challenging tasks. The risk involved was noted but there was consensus that 'If successful, the operation may have far-reaching political and morale effect' (Deputy First Sea Lord) and 'even if it is not completely successful, will have very great morale effect' (Third Sea Lord).[13] Clearly the RN's senior commanders were well aware of the psychological dimension of the raid as well as its physical potential. Their endorsement meant that an offensive against the Belgian ports was now far more likely than it had been at any previous point in the war.

The Officers of 4th Battalion Royal Marines. In the front row from left are: Capt C. B. Conybeare (wounded), Capt R. L. Del Strother (wounded), Maj C. E. C. Eagles DSO (killed), Maj A. A. Cordner (killed), LtCol B. M. Elliot DSO, Commanding Officer (killed), Capt A. R. Chater, Maj B. G. Weller DSC, Capt E. Bamford DSO, Surgeon H St C. Colson RN. Of the 19 officers in the two rear rows six were killed, four wounded and one taken prisoner. Overall the 4th Battalion suffered 366 casualties from a strength of 730, over half the total British losses in the raids. [RMM]

---

13 Keyes to the Admiralty 25 February 1918 and the Admiralty to Keyes, with Sea Lords' comment dated from the 24 February to 3 March 1918, reproduced in Halpern, Paul, *The Keyes Papers*, op. cit., pp.460–78.

THE RAID

Well before this endorsement Keyes had begun the preparations required to implement Operation Z.O. This preparation broadly fell into securing the required ships and equipment, obtaining the personnel he needed and undertaking training. Many of the wide range of what would ultimately become 165 ships and craft required to support the operation were already available locally. The monitors, destroyers, CMBs and MLs normally based at Dunkirk became the basis for the force to attack Ostend, while those from Dover formed the majority of the force for Zeebrugge. The adjacent Harwich Force was to provide the cruisers and destroyers to cover the assault and bombardment forces during their passages across the Channel.

More challenging was the assembly of the specialized shipping required for boarding and blocking operations. Keyes had at first considered using a fast merchant ship with a high freeboard as the main assault ship for the Mole but he then settled on the 6,400-ton cruiser *Vindictive*. Launched in 1897 she had served on blockade duties and off north Russia but was obsolete by 1918. She was refitted for the raid in Chatham dockyard, reducing her original armament of 6in guns in order to accommodate the specialized weapons Keyes had described in his plan. Of particular note was the conversion of the foretop into a 'fighting top' to be manned by personnel of the RMA. Armed with two 1½lb pom-poms and six Lewis guns this position would have the best field of fire to support the storming parties due to its elevated position. In addition the ship also required a series of oversize fenders to protect its port side from damage when it was alongside the Mole. A further threat when alongside was of damage to the ship's propellers. This was countered by using a length of the mainmast, which had been removed, as a propeller guard, by mounting it horizontally across the quarterdeck, projecting several feet over the port quarter. Finally a higher deck was required on the port side and this was constructed of wood from the forecastle back to the quarterdeck. Three wide ramps were built from the upper deck to the starboard side of this new deck to allow easy access for the storming

HMS *Vindictive* as adapted for the raid on Zeebrugge. This was an innovative conversion of a normal warship for an almost unheard-of assault role. Clearly visible is the wooden deck added on the ship's port side, the propeller guard on the stern and the wide range of infantry support weapons, designed to suppress the German defences during the assault. Also evident is the new foretop, armed with pom-pom cannons and Lewis machine guns. When the ship was alongside the Mole this provided the only weapons elevated above the parapet. [NHB]

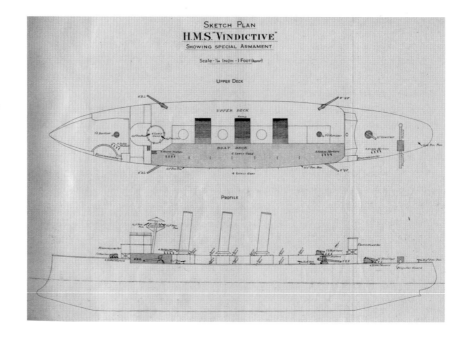

Sperrversuch gegen Zeebrügge am 23.4.18. — Großer Kreuzer „Vindictive" nach seiner Rückkehr von Zeebrügge

A post-raid picture of the starboard side of *Vindictive* which clearly shows several important adaptations. The foretop is visible forward of the funnels, with the reinforced bridge forward of that and lower. The 'hut' on the portside of the ship was the conning position used by Capt Carpenter during the final approach to the Mole. It also contained the controls for the ship's flame throwers, though the pipes for these were cut by shellfire so that they were never used. [RNM]

parties. Fourteen narrow, hinged brows were constructed on the false deck in order to bridge the gap to the Mole, the number of landing platforms addressing the vulnerability that Keyes had identified in the single wide brow of Bacon's plans. The false deck was also equipped with eight of the total of 16 Stokes mortars and ten Lewis guns belonging to the storming parties. All were intended to provide initial suppressing fire, with the Lewis guns then going ashore with their parties.

However HMS *Vindictive* could not carry the entire assault force and it was also considered prudent not to place that force in a single ship. It was decided that two further ships were needed, with one of their requirements being a high passenger capacity so that they could engage in rescue work if a major ship was sunk by a mine while on passage or by gunfire during the action. After an exhaustive search Keyes' staff officer, Capt Herbert Grant, selected the Mersey ferries *Iris* and *Daffodil*. They had a carrying capacity of 1,500 each, were doubled hulled and shallow draft, making them less vulnerable to mines, and were extremely manoeuvrable and robust, allowing them to work in close proximity with *Vindictive* alongside the Mole. Their disadvantages were their low decks and short range. These were addressed by having *Daffodil*'s stormers cross to the Mole via *Vindictive*, with those from *Iris* having to use ladders to ascend onto the parapet. The range issue was dealt with by towing the vessels for most of the passage. *Daffodil* and *Iris* were fitted out in Portsmouth dockyard and were commissioned as HMS *Daffodil* and HMS *Iris II*.

Also requiring special preparations were the five blockships, all 3,500-ton cruisers of the *Apollo* class, HMS *Sirius*, *Intrepid* and *Iphigenia* for Zeebrugge and *Brilliant* and *Thetis* for Ostend. Completed in the early 1890s they had been variously converted to minelayers and then depot ships before the raid. They were taken in hand by Chatham dockyard for conversion in mid-January to the exacting standards laid down by the Director of Naval Construction. Most of their normal fitting had to be removed and the drafts reduced to 19ft for the Zeebrugge ships and 21ft for those going to Ostend. Their armaments were reduced to the minimum, starboard guns only for the Zeebrugge ships and forward guns only for the Ostend ones, each gun with 20 rounds, so that they would have the minimum amount of explosives on board but they would be able to briefly engage defences should they need to. A protected conning and steering position was added aft to provide redundancy, with further bullet-proof protection in vital areas. Maximum concrete was required,

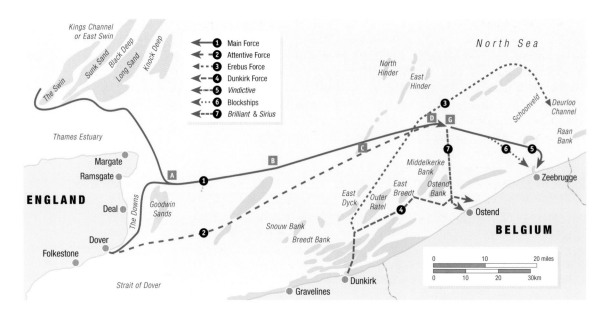

Main Force
Attentive Force
Erebus Force
Dunkirk Force
Vindictive
Blockships
Brilliant & *Sirius*

The approach of the raiders to Zeebrugge and Ostend, 22–23 April 1918.

subject to the conflicting demand for a shallow draft and stability. Through great skill around 1,000 tons of concrete, reinforced with whatever metal could be made available, including old boiler tubes, was worked into each ship. Finally four 45lb charges of TNT were placed in the double bottoms of the ships in order to sink them by blowing out their bottoms, so as to maximize the difficulties of salvage. Through strenuous efforts by Chatham dockyard all the blockships were converted by 6 March, only two days after Keyes received his approved plan back from the Admiralty and well before the first possible dates for the raid in mid-March.

The last specially converted ships required were submarines for the destruction of the Mole viaduct. This was a task in which Keyes took a particular interest, having sat on the viaduct in 1914 while assisting in the disembarkation of the British Army's 7th Division there. Having noted the strong current surging through the viaduct he had conceived of the idea of CMBs releasing rafts with high explosive that would naturally be carried onto the piers. However he was persuaded by LtCdr Francis Sandford of his staff that obsolete 300-ton coastal submarines of the C class would have better prospects of success. One would be adequate but two were taken over to provide some redundancy in the plan, C.1 and C.3. The boats were modified so that they could carry 5 tons of Amatol explosive in their bows and were fitted with gyro controls so that there was a chance of abandoning them while on their terminal course, rather than after they had struck. The crews knew however that they would probably only be able to abandon their ships, using the motor dinghy they would tow, after the submarines were lodged in the viaduct. Their commanders had fuses for five, eight and 12 minutes which they could use at their discretion.

When Keyes assumed command of the submarines it was discovered that C.3 was commanded by a married officer, so it was arranged that the unmarried Lt Richard Sandford, LtCdr Francis Sandford's younger brother, would take command. This was a reflection of both the methods and the level of detail that Keyes applied to the selection of personnel for the raid. Keyes relied heavily on officers he knew and trusted, particularly from the Gallipoli campaign, for example Cdr Henry Hardy, for key appointments, such as command of the blockships. Hardy was selected as captain of the blockship HMS *Sirius*. Trusted officers were then permitted to recommend others on whom they believed they could rely, with Admiral Beatty recommending

Lt Ivan Franks, who became the captain of HMS *Iphigenia*, and Capt Carpenter of *Vindictive*, who had twice previously served with Keyes, recommending Lt Stuart Bonham-Carter, who would command HMS *Intrepid*. (Lt Franks, however, was replaced as captain of HMS *Iphigenia* by Lt Edward Billyard-Leake shortly before the raid because of illness.) Keyes' successor as Director of Plans at the Admiralty, Capt Cyril Fall, recommended Cdr Ralph Sneyd and also liaised with the Admiralty to arrange for nominated officers to come to Dover to be interviewed by Keyes. Keyes later recorded how the interview process proceeded:

> It was very interesting to watch the reactions of the various officers – whom I interviewed singly – when I told them that the enterprise would be hazardous, and finally said that the best chance of escape I could offer them after it, was a German prison until the end of the war. With one exception only, they appeared to be simply delighted and most grateful for the honour I had done them in offering them such a wonderful prospect! Then I gave them an outline of the plan, and said that although I would make every endeavour to save them after they had sunk their ships, I felt it was a very forlorn hope. They took everything for granted, asked few questions, and went away apparently full of joy and gratitude.
>
> The one exception raised so many questions, ifs and buts, that I became impatient, and said that if he did not feel enthusiastic about it I had no wish to employ him. He made it quite clear at once that he had no intention of allowing anyone else to have his place but he would like to know what it was all for; so I told him what the submarine menace meant to the country, and how vitally important it was to use every means in our power to stop it. Finally I enlisted him, Ralph Sneyd, to lead the Zeebrugge blockships, and had every reason to be thankful for the choice.[14]

While Keyes' methods were plainly a form of patronage they also reflected the reality of the situation, where there was a premium on trying to maintain security. In order to provide the further officers required selected captains were then able to suggest two other officers whom they trusted. These methods, however, were incapable of manning the whole expedition and Keyes, ever aware of the psychological elements of the raid and the requirement to raise naval morale, determined that, 'In order that all parts of the Naval Service might share in the expedition, representative bodies of men were drawn from the Grand Fleet, the three Home Depots, the Royal Marine Artillery and Light Infantry.' Also included were small numbers of personnel from the Royal Australian Navy, the Admiralty Experimental Stations and the British Army, as well as French sailors in supporting ships. Large numbers came from the Grand Fleet with the Captain of the Fleet informing Keyes that the selection had been made in the following way:

> The Commander-in-Chief, Grand Fleet, called upon the Flag Officers commanding squadrons to provide contingents of selected volunteers from the ships under their orders. They were to be stout-hearted men, active and keen who could be depended upon in any emergency to do their very best, and having regard to the hazardous nature of the enterprise, wherever possible, unmarried or without dependents. Similarly the officers chosen were those whose powers of initiative and leadership were known to be high. The Flag Officers selected the officers and the Captains the petty officers and men.

---

14 Keyes, Sir Roger, *Naval Memoirs*, op cit., p.220.

The largest single body of extra men was drawn from the Royal Marines, who provided the 4th Battalion Royal Marines (4th RM). Originally intended to serve in Ireland it had become the reinforcement unit for the two Royal Marines Light Infantry (RMLI) battalions serving with the RND in France. In early 1918 drafting from the battalion stopped and it was concentrated at Deal for six weeks' intensive training. It was also reconstituted as a composite unit with both RMA personnel, primarily to man the various infantry support weapons on *Vindictive*, and RMLI troops, who would form part of the stormers on the Mole, together with the RN parties. Altogether there were 750 Royal Marines in the 1,780 *extra* personnel allocated to Keyes for the raid. This is often also recorded, even by the Official History and serious studies, as being the number involved in the raid but this is a misreading of Keyes' figure for the extra personnel involved. When the supporting forces, such as the destroyers and motor launches, and the bombarding and covering forces are included there would have been around 10,000 personnel at sea for the raid.

Issues of personnel and equipment for the raid were the responsibility of WgCdr Frank Brock, an officer in the RNAS when preparations for Operation Z.O. began, but in the RAF by the time the raid was launched. Keyes recorded that:

> The value of Brock's contribution to the undertaking was simply incalculable, in addition to fitting out the vessels with smoke-making apparatus, he designed special smoke floats, to be anchored in selected positions; he also designed immense flame throwers for the *Vindictive*; parachute flares for aircraft to drop; flare rockets for surface vessels to fire and special light buoys to mark the route.[15]

Brock came from the Brock Fireworks family and had already produced a wide range of technical innovations that had been significant in the war, including an incendiary bullet for use against Zeppelin airships and bright flares for the Channel barrage. His role in Operation Z.O. was pivotal because of the importance of his flameless smokescreen to the viability of penetrating the German defences. This system was a major improvement over all previous smoke-producing equipment because the cover produced had often been counter-acted by the flames required to generate the smoke. Keyes wrote that, 'When ... I first took over the preparation of this operation, it had become apparent that without an effective system of smoke-screening such an attack could hardly hope to succeed.'[16] Brock's new system abandoned the previous use of phosphorus and substituted chlorsulphonic acid, adapting a method the German Army had used earlier in the war but which he made far more effective over water. The smoke could be produced by special generators or be created by introducing the chemicals into the exhaust vents of CMBs and the funnels of destroyers. The only operational drawback was that some personnel would need to wear gas masks while smoke was being produced. However the volume of smoke required for the raid needed 82 tons of acid and there was just one manufacturer in the United Kingdom. It could only provide the acid if it ceased production of the related product, saxin, a synthetic substitute for sugar used in the management of diabetes. Ultimately a War Cabinet decision was required to secure priority for the requirements of the raid. However it was not possible to accumulate sufficient acid before the mid-March window of suitable conditions for the raid. This is often recorded as being the reason why the raid was not launched in March; however Keyes stated that the conversion

---

15 *Ibid.* pp.223 and 240.
16 Admiralty Library, *Reports on the Zeebrugge and Ostend Operations 22–23 April 1918 & Ostend Operations 10 May 1918*, Naval Intelligence Division, July 1918. This vital document includes more than 80 primary reports from the raids. Subsequent unreferenced quotes are drawn from this document.

of ships and the timing of the delivery of the Liverpool ferries meant that the March dates would not have been feasible in any case.

The delay did provide an opportunity for more training for the ships and particularly for the assault forces that would attack the Mole. The RMLI trained at Deal, the RMA practised with their wide range of weapons at Shoeburyness and the seaman assault parties honed their skills at Chatham. In the assault it was envisaged that *Vindictive* would come alongside the Mole at the far end of the Mole proper and the seamen would then assault the adjacent German guns on the Mole extension, which were assessed to be the main threat to the blockships. The RM storming parties were intended to proceed down the Mole towards the shore destroying German facilities, though the battalion's orders were clear that, 'It must be firmly impressed on all ranks that the capture of the fortified zone at the seaward end of the Mole is the first essential to ensure the success of the entire enterprise.' The training of the storming parties has been criticized, with the mixture of sailors and marines being seen as 'a curious, antique throwback to the nineteenth century and a potential source of muddle and command and control snags'. It has also been suggested that there was an overemphasis on the use of the bayonet and the application of sheer will, in a manner that seems somewhat pre-1914 in its philosophy. [17] The 4th Battalion's Order Number Two for Operation Z.O. stated that:

> Officers commanding units are to imbue their commands with the idea of carrying the operation through with the bayonet; rifle fire, machine gun fire and bomb throwing are only to be resorted to when necessary to break down enemy opposition.

This was in sharp contrast to the 'fire and movement' type of tactics that had evolved on the western front, not least among the personnel of the Royal Naval Division, which had become one of the BEF's elite formations. The mixed nature of the storming parties seems explicable given that mixed 'naval brigades' had been an entirely normal, rather than antique, procedure up until that point and very much part of most senior officers' operational experience. Sailors were also required on the Mole at the beginning of the assault in order to work the brows from *Vindictive* and generally secure the ship alongside. The mixed composition was also a result of Keyes' requirement, driven by psychology and morale, that all parts of the naval service should participate in the raid, particularly its most dramatic assault element. One of the results of this, though, was that there were few officers, certainly none of the senior officers in the storming forces, who had any recent experience of the realities of intensive fighting ashore. Keyes' submission to the Admiralty had certainly envisaged the stormers including a number who had served with the RND in order to 'augment and stiffen the force' but it seems this was not achieved, something that probably simply reflects the intensive operations the division was involved with in 1918. (The only exception regarding RND personnel involved in the raid seems to have been Surgeon Frank Pocock MC, who had served with Drake Battalion of the RND in France and was then attached to 4th RM Battalion for the raid. He later died of wounds while serving with Drake on the western front.)

The Royal Marines were trained on a tapped-out model of the Mole but were given a cover story that they were being trained for an operation in France where they would be required to assault a fortified German ammunition dump. More generally Keyes allowed 'inadvertent' disclosures of information that indicated his command were

11–12 APRIL 1918

Assault force sets out for Zeebrugge/ Ostend, but turns back after wind shift makes smokescreen impossible.

---

17 Thompson, Julian, *The Royal Marines, From Sea Soldiers to a Special Force*, Sidgwick & Jackson (London, 2000) pp.178–79.

making preparations against a German advance which might require the destruction of facilities in Calais and Dunkirk and the blocking of harbours. This sophisticated misinformation became far more convincing after the launching of Germany's major offensives in France from 21 March onwards. These offensives were initially successful, with large German advances. Germany's resources were ultimately declining, its successes involved prohibitive losses and Germany's blockaded war machine was already fatally weakened. However the advances in the spring of 1918 were the most dramatic of any army on the western front since 1914 and seemed to indicate a real threat of German victory. This was the significant new background to the final decisions regarding Operation *Z.O.* and it is important to note that the offensives put a new strain on the Dover Patrol, which was required to escort a much increased flow of troops across the Channel. Keyes was focused on not letting these new requirements disrupt preparations for the raids, which reflected both his general belief in the importance of his launching offensive action and his view that the raids were not just anti-submarine measures but were closely connected to reducing the general threat of all German attacks in the Channel, both through physical damage and by achieving psychological dominance. Had a maximum effort been made from the Flanders ports, supported by the High Seas Fleet and combined with the German Army's offensives, this could have had a significant effect. Fortunately this sort of coordination was well beyond the senior commanders of the German armed forces, though there was no way to know this and it would have been a dangerous assessment to rely on. Only minor shore bombardments were mounted by the Flanders Flotilla on the night of 20–21 March and on 9 April 1918, with no effect ashore and with two torpedo boats being lost to the Anglo-French destroyers of the Dover Patrol.

Virtually simultaneously with the second action, which would turn out to be the last surface offensive mounted by the Germans in the Channel, Keyes assembled his forces for Operation *Z.O.* Most of the warships could remain at their normal ports of Dover, Dunkirk and Harwich. The boarding and blocking forces began to gather in the West Swin Anchorage, in the northern part of the Thames Estuary, from 4 April, with the main body of Royal Marines arriving on the 6th. Here more training linked with the ships, such as rapid disembarkation, could be carried out and the isolation permitted wider briefing of the men. The disadvantages were that assault training was inevitably more restricted by ship accommodation. This was provided by the old battleship HMS *Hindustan*, later supplemented by HMS *Dominion*.

The wreck of CMB 33A just outside the canal entrance at Ostend following the failed raid attempt of 11–12 April 1918. All the crew were killed by German gunfire, it seems after the boat did not receive the general recall and so approached the coast alone. Keyes generally played down any security dangers arising from the loss of the boat, in order to not jeopardize the prospects for relaunching the raid. We now know, however, that operational maps and orders were captured from the wreck but these seem to have caused an assessment that only a raid on Ostend had been attempted and that it had been frustrated by coastal artillery. [NHB]

Also the Liverpool ferries and newly austere blockships had to be supplied with fresh water by other ships every two days due to their very limited habitability. That the raid was imminent was apparent to all when Keyes issued a secret General Order on 7 April which restated his belief that the ports were 'a constant and ever-increasing menace to the communications of our army and to the trade and food supply of our country'. He noted that the force was 'thoroughly representative of our Service' and was confident that 'all ranks will strive to emulate the heroic deeds of our brothers of the sister Service in France and Flanders'.

It was a great relief for the entire force when it first sailed at 1600hrs on 11 April to make the 63-mile approach to Zeebrugge and Ostend. The speed of the ships meant that the first few hours of the approach would have to be made in daylight and so coverage from the air against detection by German scout aircraft was vital. The 61st and 65th Wings of the ten-day-old RAF provided the air escort and bombed the targets as a diversion on the night of 11–12 April, as part of wider pattern of bombing and monitor bombardments that were aimed at making the defenders accustomed to these forms of attack as their expectation whenever there was an alert. The various components of the force were accurately navigated across the Channel and reached 'D' buoy, the fourth of the illuminated buoys laid specially to support the raid and the main point of dispersal for the different assault groups off the Flanders coast. However, at this point the wind shifted to blow from the south and so it was not possible to deploy the smokescreen. Keyes was faced with the dilemma of whether to proceed. He later wrote:

> I went through a pretty difficult time during the next few moments. I knew that every man in the expedition felt, as I did, keyed up for the ordeal. How they would hate to be called off and then asked to undergo it all over again – or perhaps worse still, have to go back to their ships having achieved nothing; we might have been seen by an enemy submarine; we knew that the Swin force had been seen by neutrals, and that if the Admiralty thought for a moment that the expedition would no longer be a surprise, they would be absolutely certain to declare it off. What would our feelings be, if the weather proved favourable after turning back. These thoughts crowded through my mind and I was horribly tempted. It would be so much easier to go on and trust to the God of Battles and the good fortune of the British Navy for a happy issue.[18]

However, knowing the centrality of an effective smokescreen to any real chance of success, Keyes decided to withdraw and the force turned back with the loss of one CMB in a collision. As the ships turned a salvo of 30.5cm shells, probably directed by sound ranging, fell just 200 yards from Keyes' flagship, the destroyer HMS *Warwick*. Keyes would later learn that two of the RAF bombers and CMB 33A of

Vice-Admiral Keyes' flagship for both raids, the destroyer HMS *Warwick*. Built by Hawthorn Leslie in 1917, this ship displaced approximately 1,500 tons, could achieve over 30 knots and had a crew of 135. *Warwick* was armed with four 4in guns and six torpedo tubes, as well as a minelaying capacity. Though badly damaged by a mine during the return from Ostend in May 1918, *Warwick* was successfully repaired and served into World War II. [NHB]

18 Keyes, Sir Roger, *Naval Memoirs*, op. cit., pp.252–53.

the Ostend force were also missing. Refusing to be discouraged Keyes immediately had the units reinstated to their launch positions and on 13 April, the last opportunity in the April window of conditions, he again made the preparatory signal. Again the special navigation buoys were laid but soon the weather was too rough for the minor craft or to allow boarding ships to lie alongside the Mole. Keyes ordered the force to sail anyway in the hope that conditions might improve but was forced to again issue the recall, this time after only two hours, when the weather did not abate. There was now the prospect of trying to maintain both the force and surprise until the next window of possibly suitable conditions in May.

Keyes' thoughts on the initial cancellation show he was well aware of the difficulties of maintaining security for three weeks now that the force had been assembled and widely briefed. He was also aware that doubts about security might well lead the Admiralty to cancel the raid and disperse the force, particularly given the high demand for Channel escorts. He may have also feared that the men of his RM landing force might be taken for the desperate fighting ashore, in the same way as the amphibiously trained 1st Division had been taken in October 1917 for Passchendaele. Equally the more intensive fighting ashore is likely to have increased his determination that the Royal Navy must be seen to be undertaking any offensive operation, whatever the risks, in order to demonstrate its equal commitment alongside the army.

When the First Sea Lord arrived, shortly after the second cancellation, ready to disperse the force, Keyes therefore made a new proposal, stating that he would not need to delay by three weeks but only by nine or ten days. This would mean launching the raid with a high enough tide but under a full moon, rather than on a dark night, one of Keyes' own previous preconditions. Instead he now increasingly stressed the significance of smoke cover rather than darkness as the key condition for a reasonable chance of success. While Admiral Weymss was undoubtedly initially sceptical he was also well aware of the wider situation, particularly the desperate situation of the army, and the possible operational and strategic advantages of the raid. He was therefore able to assess the increased risk that was now being proposed in context. In this situation he ensured that the Admiralty consented to an early remounting of the raid on a moonlit night. Keyes made minor amendments to improve the plan in

HMS *Terror*, a 15in gun monitor, commissioned in August 1916, which spent the whole of its World War I service with the Dover Patrol. *Terror*'s first bombardment of the Belgium coast was on 16 August 1916 and the last on 16 October 1918. Damaged by a mine off Dunkirk in 1917, *Terror* was back with the Dover Patrol in January 1918 and was an important bombardment ship for the raid on Zeebrugge, driving the defenders to seek shelter and covering the noise of the approaching raiders. After the raid *Terror* carried out a subsequent bombardment which hit a lock gate on 9 June, disabling the canal for the rest of June and therefore causing more physical disruption to the Germans than the raid itself. HMS *Terror* again served with distinction off North Africa in 1940–41 before being sunk by aircraft on 24 February 1941. [NHB]

the light of the force's new experience and to try to minimize the impact of future weather. Smoke-making equipment was installed on more destroyers so that adequate smoke could still be made even if the weather forced MLs and CMBs to turn back. Only the MLs with volunteer crews detailed to recover the blockship crews would continue regardless and Keyes envisaged the blockships going in even if the weather was too rough for the boarding ships to go alongside the Mole. His greatest emphasis was now on smoke and on 19 April he told the force that, while he would not launch the raid if the wind was unsuitable for the smokescreen, if the force was committed and the wind was then to change he expected the smoke-making ships to be prepared 'to make smoke very close inshore, and the success of the Operation will depend on the resource and initiative of the small craft concerned'. The force now awaited the first possible sailing date to match the new tidal window, 22 April.

On the other side of the Channel the MarineKorps Flandern was also waiting, as it had been for over three years, countering bombing and shelling but never required to repel an actual attack, though the formation's historian commented that 'the dread spectre of the landing haunted the coast'. The MarineKorps had to be prepared for a wide range of possible attacks and indeed much of their planning effort went into 'Fall K', a contingency operation to cope with an attack resulting from a British invasion of Holland, an event the German Naval Staff thought quite feasible. However Von Schroder did not neglect the possibility of a direct attack on the coast and in June 1917 he had given his command the following, generally shrewd assessment:

The main object of hostile enterprises against the Coast of Flanders is to paralyse the submarine warfare. This may be accomplished by the following means:-

1. Destruction of Zeebrugge and Ostend by bombardment from the sea. Main objective: Lock at Zeebrugge ...

2. Raids by landing parties with the same object. Attempts to block the harbour entrances.

3. Landing by large masses of troops for the capture of the coast, probably accompanied by simultaneous attack on the land front of the Marine Korps, and possibly also from Holland [This possibility was then largely discounted because of the strength of the coast defences].

...

Enterprise under heads 1 and 2 must always be considered possible. They will generally take the form of a surprise, especially in hazy weather, by night and about dawn.

...

In all cases defence is primarily the duty of the Coast Artillery. In the closest co-operation with sea and air forces it attacks by fire every enemy appearing within effective range. It prevents the approach of enemy ships, and seeks to prevent destruction by hostile long-range fire of our coast establishments, if necessary, by fire at extreme ranges.

The number and calibre of the guns and the ammunition supply, which is liberally suited to their life, are equal to meeting an attack by powerful fleets for several days.

22 APRIL 1918

2310hrs Smokescreen laid prior to assault.

22 APRIL 1918

2330hrs Bombardment of harbour begins.

> If the enemy approaches by night, a belt of star shell on any desired frontage can be put
> down at about 5km [3 miles] from the coast. At shorter ranges this star-shell barrage
> is supplemented by numerous searchlights.

This assessment was supplemented by a further set of 'hand-over' notes of October 1917, intended for units as they rotated through the coastal defences. After repeating the central arguments of the previous paper it went on to state that:

> In the sector of the 1st Naval Division, from the Dutch Border to Raversijde (6 km
> [3¾ miles] to the West of Ostend), 26 batteries have been erected for the repulse of
> hostile operations, which in the main are grouped round the two most important points
> of the coast – Zeebrugge and Ostend.

These batteries ranged from 8.8cm (3.5in) to 38cm (15in) guns with ranges of up to 40,000m (43,745 yards); these guns were 'the backbone of the defence' and the emphasis was on destroying enemy ships at long range, utilizing land and air spotting when possible and sound ranging at night and when visibility was poor.[19]

While the German forces were on constant watch they had noticed an increase in air and sea bombardments in the spring of 1918. On the night of 11–12 April engine noises at sea had been detected, followed by the shore bombardment from 0015hrs. Shortly afterwards a single CMB appeared close inshore off Ostend and was destroyed by gunfire, the crew being killed. The wrecked vessel was however salvaged and operational maps and orders were found on board. This was the fate of the missing CMB 33A, a loss which had been played down by Keyes. Von Schroder's interpretation of the intelligence, which was fairly explicit about a likely attack on Ostend but implicit about any assault on Zeebrugge, was significant for the final raid. He decided that the operation had been aimed only at Ostend and that the strength of the coastal artillery had forced the British to abandon the operation at some distance, in line with the expectations set out in his papers above. Aerial reconnaissance seemed to confirm his belief when it revealed concentrations of shipping in Dover and Dunkirk the following day. Von Schroder raised the state of the coastal alert in general, but he raised it specifically only at Ostend, not at Zeebrugge. He also decided not to increase night patrol craft, partly because he assessed that he had too few craft to make the patrols effective and partly because he feared their possible presence might inhibit the coastal artillery that was so central to his defence.

On 22 April, the first day of the new window of acceptable tide conditions, the weather was also adequate and Keyes ordered that the raid be mounted. The first ships left the Swin anchorage at 1300hrs and joined the Dover forces by 1700hrs, all the daytime movements again having an air escort against discovery of RAF scout aircraft. Before dark Keyes made the following general signal to the force, 'St George for England', provoking the famous reply from Capt Carpenter of *Vindictive*, 'May we give the dragon's tail a damned good twist.'[20] Although there was a bright full moon, visibility was soon reduced to about 1 mile by mist and drizzle. Although these conditions were very valuable for the final approach they were a further challenge to an already ambitious requirement for the navigation and coordination of this large and complex force, including large numbers of vessels under tow. This was a point where the underlying professionalism and the extended sea time of the crews paid dividends, particularly as they had been boosted with extensive rehearsals, which had considered

19 Von Schroder as reproduced in Admiralty Library *The Report of Committee Appointed to Examine The German Defences on the Belgian Coast* (1919) pp.7–14.
20 Keyes, Sir Roger, *Naval Memoirs*, op. cit., p.262

A German mobile 150cm searchlight photographed after the withdrawal from Flanders. These searchlights were an important element of the integrated defence of the Flanders coast against both ships and aircraft. Their attempts to illuminate the raiders, in order to allow accurate gunnery against them, were largely frustrated by the British smokescreens until the raid was well underway. [NHB]

the widest possible range of contingencies, allowing signalling to be minimized. These preparations were then combined with the programme of specially illuminated navigation buoys, once again laid across the Channel especially for the operation. These marked points A, B, C, D, E (no F) and G on passage. On arrival at point 'C' Keyes assessed that the wind, blowing from the north-east towards the land, was favourable for the smokescreens, and so a short wireless signal indicated to the whole force that the raid was proceeding. Position 'G' marked a 2-mile gap in the net barrage off the Belgian coast that the force could proceed through and was also the point where surplus passage crews were removed from the blockships and the CMBs were released from their tows.

At 2310hrs on 22 April the various craft began to lay the vital smokescreen, with the faster CMBs laying the first smoke so that slower MLs could work under its cover. The smoke consisted of both general screens off the harbours, which ultimately extended for 8 miles, and particular concentrations at certain key points. At Zeebrugge this meant laying intensive smoke just off the Mole to screen *Vindictive*'s approach as well as arranging the screen with deliberate but narrow gaps that would assist the final navigation of the boarding and blockships. Lt Edward Hill was the commanding officer of CMB 35A and was detailed to lay smoke off the western side of the Mole. His boat fouled its propeller while on tow with the main force and had to be towed by a drifter back to Dover. Clearing the propeller by 2140hrs he proceeded across the Channel at full speed to arrive 1 mile off the Mole by 2320hrs and commence laying smoke to the west of the Mole, increasingly using the smoke from his own smoke floats to cover him as German searchlights and fire increased. CMB 23B laid smoke just off the Mole to try to screen *Vindictive* and after she came alongside laid more in an attempt to screen the blockships from the German guns on the Mole extension. As the action increased more and more smoke floats were sunk by German gunnery and the method of adding chemicals to the exhausts of the craft was used to increase the smoke.

One of the most important reasons that these craft were able to lay the smokescreen related to the long-range fire which had been opened by the 15in gun monitors HMS *Erebus* and HMS *Terror* from around 2330hrs.[21] It had been hoped

---

21 British and German primary sources give the commencement of the bombardment at various times ranging from 2320hrs to 2335hrs.

EVENTS ▼

1 The site of the intensive fighting on the Mole. It was in this area that the raiders made desperate efforts to advance towards the gun battery on the Mole Extension. During these assaults Capt Edward Bamford RMLI, Able Seaman Albert McKenzie RN and Lt Cdr Arthur Harrison RN all won the VC. Lt Cdr Harrison's award was posthumous. Despite having been wounded onboard *Vindictive* he continued to lead a party of sailors ashore and launched an attack on towards the German guns where every participant was killed or wounded.

2 The self-destruction of the submarine C.3. C.3 had been successfully rammed into the viaduct connecting the Mole to the shore by its crew and exploded at approximately 0020hrs, severing the Mole from the land. The explosion of five tons of Amatol was enormous but several participants recorded that the fighting was so intense that, though they saw the flash, they did not hear the explosion.

GERMAN DEFENCES **1 – 3**

1 The Friedrichsort Battery
2 German torpedo boat, V.69
3 Net barrier across canal entrance

LOCATIONS **1 – 3**

1 The Mole extension
2 The canal entrance
3 Planned position for HMS *Vindictive* and HMS *Daffodil*

BRITISH FORCES **1 – 8**

1 HMS *Vindictive*
2 HMS *Daffodil*
3 HMS *Thetis*
4 HMS *Intrepid*
5 HMS *Iphigenia*
6 Royal Navy Motor Launches
7 Royal Navy Coastal Motor Boats
8 HMS *Iris II*

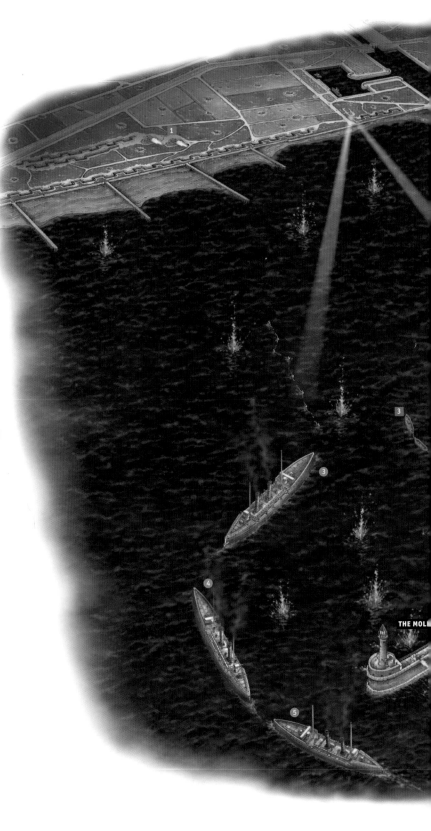

THE MOLE

THE RAID ON ZEEBRUGGE

0020 HRS, 23 APRIL 1918

ENTRANCE

PLANNED POSITION FOR
HMS *VINDICTIVE* AND HMS *DAFFODIL*

A post-raid photograph of HMS *Vindictive*. The damaged brows are visible on the port side and the foretop mounted on the mast can be seen just above the bridge. Towards the stern can be seen one of the alternative conning positions that provided redundancy for steering the ship during the raid. [RNM]

that this bombardment could be combined with air attack but the cloud and mist that was assisting the raiders also prevented the RAF attack or its planned later illumination of the harbour. The monitors were less weather dependent and their shells were sufficient to initially convince the German command that this was another of the regular long-range bombardments, with the result that most of the local garrisons and ships' crews took shelter rather than manned defences, giving the approaching raiders the vital minutes which allowed them to proceed well within the range of the coastal guns without loss.

At around 2345hrs three CMBs passed down the seaward side of the Mole in order to bring it under fire with Stokes mortars, the object being to suppress any defenders before *Vindictive* arrived. Simultaneously CMB 5 and CMB 7 attacked the harbour side of the Mole with the object of destroying any German torpedo boats or destroyers alongside, which could potentially torpedo the blockships during their final approach. Only one ship, the destroyer V.69, was present. It was attacked, with SubLt Blake of CMB 7 reporting that:

> [At 2347hrs] ... in accordance with previous orders, parted company with main force, and proceeded on a course S.33 E. in direction of Zeebrugge Mole Lighthouse at a speed of approximately 25 knots. At 1151 sighted Zeebrugge Mole Lighthouse about 4 points on port bow, distance 150 yards. No.7 then altered course so as to pass close to the end of Mole, losing sight of No.5 in the smoke. On arriving abeam of Mole, closed harbour boom, and with the help of enemy star shells, followed it down till an opening was observed close in shore. Helm was then put hard-a-port and out-clutch so as to observe some target to aim at. Enemy star shells NW of Mole silhouetted an enemy destroyer apparently secured to the Mole just to the west of No.3 shed. I then proceeded to work up to 30 knots and fired torpedo at a range of about 600 yards, point of aim amidships. Boat was then stopped to observe result. Observed hit in line with forebridge. Having observed torpedo, altered course to port so as to escape to eastward and make smoke as ordered ... during this time I was heavily fired upon by machine-guns on Mole and heavy batteries to eastward of canal.

SubLt Blake's CMB ultimately returned to Dover under tow, having been damaged when it struck a buoy in the harbour. In reality no damage had been done to V.69 and the fire from the various attacks was initially thought to be part of the general bombardment. However the defenders were starting to realize that something more than shelling was happening as they were beginning to hear the engine noises. Between about 2345hrs and 2355hrs the Mole's various batteries and defences were manned and the coastal batteries began to lay down a barrage on pre-planned zones just outside the harbour.

Remarkably the raiders had now penetrated a defensive zone that extended over nearly 25 miles and were only a few hundred yards from their first target. As the official history puts it, 'The entire expedition had reached its destination unreported and unobserved.'[22] However as the Germans manned their defences the wind was also changing direction, turning to blow from the south, so pushing the smoke towards the attackers and away from the defenders. As a result the Mole defenders reported seeing a large ship loom out of the smoke at approximately 2356hrs. This was *Vindictive*. Capt Carpenter later recorded that visibility just before this 'can hardly have amounted to a yard – the forecastle was invisible from the bridge' but then the ship passed through the smoke and the Mole became visible as estimated 300 yards away:

> Course was altered immediately to the south-westward and speed was increased to the utmost.

> The Mole battery opened fire at once: our own guns, under the direction of Commander E. O. B. S. Osbourne, replied with the utmost promptitude. The estimated distance at which we passed the Mole battery was 250 yards off the eastern gun, gradually reducing to 50 yards off the western gun. It was truly a wonderful sight. The noise was terrific and the flashes of the Mole guns seemed to be within arm's length. Of course it was, to all intents and purposes, impossible for the Mole guns to miss their target. They literally poured projectiles into us. In about five minutes we had reached the Mole, but not before the ship had suffered a great amount of damage to both material and personnel.[23]

As *Vindictive* came alongside the Mole at 0001hrs, only one minute after the planned time, the German guns could no longer come to bear on her, exactly as had been planned, and the ship had suffered no fundamental damage to her hull or engines. Carpenter attributed this to the short distance involved, which encouraged rapid and crudely aimed fire from the German guns and the effect of the counter-fire from the ship's gunners.

The damage and disruption that *Vindictive* had suffered was still very serious. Many of the ship's gunners had been killed, with the forward 7.5in howitzer having

British CMBs at Dunkirk before the raid on Zeebrugee. The short range of the boats put a premium on basing them as close to the enemy as possible or they had to be towed towards their objectives, a system only possible in reasonably calm weather. Noticeable on the boats are the red-white-blue recognition roundels, more commonly associated with aircraft. One of the boats clearly shows a Stokes mortar on deck, identifying it as one of those detailed to attack the Mole immediately before HMS *Vindictive* landed her raiders. [NHB]

22 Newbolt, Henry, *Naval Operations, Volume V*, Longman (London, 1931) p.255.
23 Carpenter, Alfred, *The Blocking of Zeebrugge*, Herbert Jenkins (London, 1925) pp.190–91.

PREVIOUS PAGES
Sgt Norman Finch of the RMA winning the Victoria Cross (VC) in the foretop of HMS *Vindictive*. The foretop provided vital suppressing fire in support of the raiders storming the Mole but was terribly exposed to German fire and was hit many times. One shell killed or wounded all the occupants but, with complete disregard for his survival, the injured Sgt Finch continued to provide vital supporting fire with a Lewis gun until that was also disabled. He then assisted the wounded Gunner Sutton to the deck before collapsing from his own wounds. Sgt Finch was awarded his VC under Rule 13 of the Victoria Cross Regulations which allowed for a ballot of a unit after a particularly arduous action. The regulations provided for separate ballots by rank but a ballot was actually held across all the ranks with Finch and Capt Edward Bamford being selected. From *Vindictive* Capt Carpenter and Able Seaman Albert McKenzie were selected. All those eligible for the ballot had that fact noted in their service records. Finch served with the Royal Marines from 1908 to 1929 and again from 1939 to 1943, and was part of the Honour Guard for the internment of the Unknown Warrior in Westminster Abbey in 1920.

two complete crews killed or wounded before it was abandoned, and the fuel pipes to the flame thrower had been cut. This reduced the amount of supporting fire for the landing. The landing parties had also suffered, with LtCol Elliott of the Royal Marines and his second-in-command both killed, as well as Capt Halahan who commanded the naval landing parties. All had been in exposed positions waiting to lead their men ashore. Also the increase in speed to minimize the time under fire meant *Vindictive* had come alongside about 300 yards further down the Mole than intended, meaning the stormers were now that distance from their target battery. Finally the fire had destroyed many of the brows, and only two were operational, with two more later being brought back into working order.

Even the use of these brows was doubtful as *Vindictive* had difficulties in securing steadily alongside, fighting the current flowing between her and the Mole. For several minutes naval personnel made Herculean efforts to secure the ship with enormous grappling irons or 'Mole anchors' designed to grip the parapet wall. These were ultimately inadequate by themselves and Carpenter later described this period, with dramatic understatement, as 'a very trying period'. Only through HMS *Daffodil* coming up and 'nudging' *Vindictive* alongside at a right angle was *Vindictive* able to remain alongside, *Daffodil*'s landing parties proceeding through *Vindictive*. LtCdr Harrison led the storming parties, despite having had his jaw broken by a shell-splinter, ashore but the reality of landing was still a daunting prospect:

> The difficulty of getting along a narrow and extremely unsteady brow whilst fully accoutred, the fact that the men on the brow were under heavy machine-gun fire from close range, and the presence of a thirty-foot drop between the Mole and the ship ensuring almost certain death, were enough to make the bravest man hesitate. Nevertheless, the storming of the Mole ... was carried out without the smallest delay, and without any apparent consideration of self-preservation.

Sgt Harry Wright of the Royal Marines described the reality of landing:

> Up the ramp we dashed, carrying our ladders and ropes, passing our dead and wounded lying everywhere and big gaps made in the ship's decks by shell fire, finally crossing the two remaining gangways which were only just hanging together. We jumped on to the concrete wall only to find it swept with machine-gun fire.

Our casualties were so great before the landing that out of a platoon of 45 men only 12 landed.[24]

The stormers found it impossible to make enough progress towards the seaward end of the Mole to knock out the gun battery there that was their first priority, with the closest parties approaching the junction of the Mole and the Mole extension by the time the recall was sounded. The automatic fire from the Mole defences and the guns of V.69, manned by both the Mole garrison and the torpedo boat's crew, made any progress very difficult. However some of the raiders were able get down from the exposed parapet and establish positions across the width of the Mole, fully engaging the defenders and repelling counter-attacks, thus fulfilling the requirement to occupy the defences, though with desperately heavy casualties, including WgCdr Brock, who had persuaded Keyes to let him land to inspect German sound-ranging technology. In achieving their success in occupying the defences the raiders were greatly assisted and encouraged by the supporting fire from the fore or 'fighting' top that had been created on *Vindictive*. Positioned above the Mole it was able to fire down onto the defenders but in return was terribly exposed to their fire. Around 20 minutes into the action the foretop received a direct hit from V.69 on the other side of the Mole. All the RMA gunners were killed or wounded but Sgt Norman Finch, despite being wounded, continued firing his Lewis gun until the foretop was hit again and finally destroyed as a viable firing point. Sgt Finch was one of the 11 raiders later awarded the Victoria Cross.

While this fighting was going on desperate efforts were being made to land more stormers from HMS *Iris II*, which by 0015hrs was anchored ahead of *Vindictive* but with her deck much lower from the parapet. LtCdr Bradford climbed a derrick in order to secure a parapet anchor but was shot while achieving this and fell between the ship and the Mole. Lt Hawkings managed to climb a ladder and reached the parapet but at this point *Iris II*'s No.1 anchor tore away and the ship surged away from the Mole. Lt Hawkings was last seen firing his revolver on the Mole. Cdr Gibbs decided to bring *Iris II* alongside *Vindictive* to disembark but this was only achieved shortly before the recall so few of his stormers ever made it on to the Mole.

The scale of casualties tested the medical arrangements for the raid, with much of the burden falling on Staff Surgeon James McCutcheon, the Senior Medical Officer in *Vindictive*. He had a team of just over 30, mostly volunteer ratings and two other surgeons. Stretcher parties were placed under the supervision of Chaplain Peshall, medical stores were cached throughout likely points of need on the ship and every man on board was supplied with a dressing. McCutcheon later wrote that:

At 11.50 pm the first batch of wounded began to arrive, and from then until the '*Vindictive*' left the Mole the stream of casualties was continuous, and it was soon found necessary to utilise the ward room, aft deck, sick bay, all cabins, and, in fact all available space of the ship between decks for the disposal of the wounded.

At 1.15 am we left the Mole, and from then until about 10 am, when we arrived at the disembarkation pier at Dover, medical officers, sick-berth ratings, stretcher parties, and voluntary assistants of all ranks were fully occupied in attending to the needs of the wounded.

Most of the cases had multiple wounds of an extensive nature, accompanied by severe

OPPOSITE
A form of personnel bunker, built against the outer wall of the Mole. This type included elevated machine-gun positions which were one of the keys to the stubborn German defence and virtually impossible for the raiders to silence with the infantry weapons at their disposal. HMS *Vindictive*'s position further along the Mole from the Mole extension meant the raiders were subject to more firepower from these positions than had been expected. [NHB]

---

24 Wright, Harry, *Memoirs of Sergeant Harry Wright (Zeebrugge & Aftermath)*, Royal Marines Historical Society (Portsmouth, 1990) p.8.

haemorrhage, which had been caused by bullet, shrapnel, high explosive, or what appeared to be an explosive bullet.

Of the 900 personnel in *Vindictive* 60 were killed and 176 wounded, five of whom died before reaching Dover. Keyes later wrote that, 'no branch of the service surpassed in zeal and ability the efforts of the medical branch to prove itself worthy of its profession'.

One element of the Mole plan which did succeed very much as intended was the submarine attack on the viaduct. Two submarines, C.1 and C.3, were prepared for the role and were towed across the Channel. C.1 lost her tow and took no further part in the operation but C.3 continued, demonstrating the value of the redundancy measures built into the plan. C.3 approached the Mole, coming under intermittent illumination and fire. The ship tried to generate a smokescreen but was frustrated by the change of wind. The commanding officer, Lt Sandford, reported that:

> When 100 yards from viaduct, course was altered to N. 85 degrees E to ensure striking exactly at right angles, and collision with the viaduct took place at 9½ knots almost immediately afterwards. ...

> The boat stuck exactly between two rows of piles, and penetrated to the conning tower, riding up on to the horizontal girders of the viaduct, and the hull being raised from the water bodily about 2ft thereby.

> The skiff was then lowered and manned by the crew, who had mustered on deck previous to the collision taking place.

> The fuses were then ignited and the submarine abandoned, course being set to the westward against the current. The propeller of the skiff having been damaged oars only could be used. Immediately on the skiff leaving the submarine two searchlights were switched on and fire was opened with machine-guns, rifles and pom-poms. The boat being penetrated many times, but being kept afloat with a pump which had been fortunately fitted. I was myself wounded and then two of the crew.

> The charge [5 tons of Amatol] exploded when the skiff was only 200–300 yards from the viaduct, as little progress could be made against the current ... The effect of the explosion appeared to be great, much debris falling to the water around.

Fortunately one of the side effects of the explosion was that the searchlights and firing became less intense and the crew of C.3 were recovered by a picket boat. It is a sign of the general intensity of the fighting on the Mole that many of those present later recalled the flash of C.3's explosion but could not hear the noise it made over the sound of the fighting.

Given the enormous effort and sacrifice being made on the Mole, and that the bulk of the force was being applied there, it is easy almost to overlook the fact that all this activity was subsidiary and intended to support to the success of the blocking ships. C.3 exploded at around 0020hrs just as HMS *Thetis* approached the Mole, unscathed but coming under fire from the guns on the Mole extension, exactly as had been anticipated. She returned fire and though damaged continued into the harbour but was unable to manoeuvre to avoid the net barrier in front of her, possibly as a result of damage to her steering. The nets gradually fouled both her propellers and *Thetis* lost way about 300 yards short of the canal entrance and well short of her

23 APRIL 1918

0001hrs HMS *Vindictive* comes alongside the Mole.

23 APRIL 1918

0020hrs C.3 explodes.

The gap in the viaduct caused by the explosion of the Royal Navy submarine C.3. This photograph is taken from the landward side, showing the curve of the Mole in the background. While the walkway shown in the photo was quickly assembled, substantial repairs took far longer and the goal of isolating the Mole during the raid was achieved completely. [NHB]

target of the lock gates, with Cdr Sneyd signalling the following ships to pass her. The crew then managed to get the starboard shaft briefly operating and swung the ship back into the Channel where she was scuttled, the crew evacuating in a cutter and being picked up by ML 526.

The following blockships benefited from the passage of *Thetis* in that she had cleared the net obstacle and absorbed the bulk of the fire from the coastal guns. Lt Bonham-Carter recorded that as he approached the Mole there was some shrapnel but this was useless due to the smoke cover and as he approached the canal, 'We had very few guns firing at us, the enemy appearing to concentrate entirely on the Mole and HMS *Thetis*.' The diversion on the Mole had therefore succeeded in its main purpose, with the crew of V.69 fighting on the Mole and unable to launch any torpedoes. *Intrepid* now had a clear run as far as the vital lock gate. However it seems the orders had not explicitly addressed the issue of whether *Intrepid* should ram the gates if possible, should *Thetis* have failed to do so, and Lt Bonham-Carter reported that 'orders were carried out as nearly as possible' by sinking his ship in the canal entrance:

> After getting to my position I went full speed ahead starboard, full speed astern port, helm hard a starboard. I then waited for the crews to get into the boats but finding the ship was coming astern I had to blow her up ... I then left the compass platform and launched with four P.O.s, Lt Cory-Wright and Sub-Lt Babb a Carley raft and proceeded down the canal. We were picked up by ML 282 who came right in under the stem of '*Iphigenia*'. This motor launch, which was under heavy fire from machine guns, undoubtedly was the cause of us being picked up. Her commanding officer, Lt Dean RNVR, was simply magnificent.

Bonham-Carter's crew had amounted to 87 as he had been unable to remove his passage crew at 'D' buoy but incredibly only one was killed in the ML during their rescue, all the others surviving.

The final blockship, HMS *Iphigenia*, had a similar approach to *Intrepid* but was hit twice and blinded by smoke and escaping steam as she entered the canal. Lt Billyard-Leake believed *Intrepid* was blocking the western side of the canal with her stern but there was a gap between the eastern side and her bow. He tried to close this but struck *Intrepid*'s bow, compromising her position but ultimately driving his bows into the eastern bank and then scuttling the ship. *Iphigenia*'s crew were also rescued from the ship's cutter by ML 282, which now carried 101 survivors, an incredible load for a craft of 34 tons with a normal complement of eight. Lt Dean's

Lieutenant Stuart Bonham-Carter, the last man to leave his ship, HMS *Intrepid*, as it sank as a blockship in the canal entrance at Zeebrugge. *Intrepid* had arrived at this point with far more sailors onboard than had been expected, as it had not been possible to remove the spare engine room 'stokers' at Point 'D' during the passage. This meant that Bonham-Carter and the last of his crew abandoned ship into a Carley Float, as shown at the bottom of the ladder. This was a basic rescue raft and it was fortunate they were soon recovered by ML 282. Bonham-Carter has sometimes been criticized for his failure to ram the lock gate, visible beyond the ship's bow. However it was Admiral Keyes' orders that did not set a clear priority between ramming the gate and scuttling in the canal entrance, in order to cause silting up of the channel. Keyes would later regret this. Bonham-Carter had been commissioned as a sub-lieutenant in 1908 and continued to serve into World War II, becoming a vice-admiral and Flag Officer Malta in 1942–43. Retiring at the end of 1943, he continued to serve as a convoy commodore, controlling merchant ships for the remainder of the war.

steering gear then jammed but he manoeuvred the launch with the engines, working close to the Mole to avoid enemy fire as he left the harbour and then transferred the survivors to HMS *Warwick*. When the sailors realized they were being transferred to Keyes' flagship they burst into cheers.

With the expenditure of the blockships the raid had achieved as much as it could. Capt Carpenter had observed all the blockships pass the Mole, none of his guns that could bear directly on the Mole were operational and his ship was being hit several times a minute. Appreciating that little demolition was likely to be happening on the Mole he sounded the recall, having to use *Daffodil*'s whistle, as his own had been destroyed. He waited for several minutes after the flow of returning raiders had halted and then left at 0110hrs. As the ships left the shelter of the Mole wall *Iris II* was hit heavily by multiple shells and as she was packed with men the casualties were very heavy, including her commanding officer, Cdr Gibbs. *Iris II* was saved by the professional and gallant conduct of the crew and by an emergency smokescreen placed by ML 558. Her experienced medical officer, Surgeon Frank Pocock MC, attended the overwhelming number of casualties during the return voyage until the ship reached Dover at 1445hrs: 'He had all the work to do himself, as all his staff were killed. His work certainly saved many lives.' For his conduct Surgeon Pocock was admitted to the DSO.

Fortunately *Iris II*'s losses in the retirement proved to be the exception but the German gunners were now demonstrating their potential on any other closing opportunity. When the destroyer HMS *North Star* emerged from the smokescreen near the Mole at 0055hrs her commanding officer saw an opportunity to try to torpedo ships alongside the Mole. He fired three torpedoes but as the ship passed close by the lighthouse to leave the harbour she was hit by multiple shells which destroyed the engine room and boilers. The ship was stopped just 400 yards from the Mole by 0125hrs. The destroyer HMS *Phoebe* closed between *North Star* and the shore and made a new smokescreen. Incredibly maximum effort was made for nearly an hour to save *North Star* before *Phoebe* finally left the harbour entrance at around 0225hrs, marking the effective end of the raid on Zeebrugge.

The parallel raid on Ostend followed a similar though simplified methodology but met with less success. Again there was a programme of distant bombardment, in this attack including long-range land-based guns, with the weather preventing bombing or air marking with flares. Next a smokescreen was laid by minor craft which then stood by to rescue the crews of the blockships, in this case the cruisers *Sirius* and *Brilliant*. There was no Mole at Ostend to bar the canal entrance but neither was there any prominent landmark to indicate it. The smokescreen worked well but the wind then reversed and blew it back out to sea just as the blockships were approaching the coast and all the RN ships were subject to very heavy fire from the Ostend batteries, which were on a higher state of alert than those at Zeebrugge. When the blockships were on their final approach to the shore they fixed their position from the German-controlled Stroom Bank Buoy. Although they made an accurate correction for the normal position of the buoy they were unaware that the Germans had moved the buoy, with the result that both blockships went aground 2,400 yards east of the eastern pier of the canal. Cdre Hubert Lynes, the commander for this element of Operation Z.O., believed the buoy had been moved in response to the aborted raid of 11–12 April and regretted that air reconnaissance of the coast had not been undertaken after that date. However German sources show that the buoy had been moved 1 mile east only the night before as part of normal defensive measures used occasionally in Flanders. The aground blockships were destroyed and the crews rescued by MLs without further loss.

Keyes determined to follow up this obvious failure at Ostend, which would mitigate apparent success at Zeebrugge, with a second raid. He intended to use the battered *Vindictive* and launch the new raid only four days after the first. *Vindictive* was patched together and loaded with 200 tons of cement for 27 April but the weather was then unfavourable and the raid had to wait until a suitably high night tide at Ostend, with the timing allowing the force to escape before dawn. This became an increasingly challenging combination as the nights shortened. The night of 9–10 May was selected as the new target date and this allowed another old cruiser, HMS *Sappho*, now being used as a depot ship but similar to the previous blockships, to be prepared. The officers of the original blockships were reappointed to the new ones but with new crews of volunteers drawn from the Dover Patrol. The plan had some similarities to the previous raid but it was decided to commence shelling only once the approaching ships had been discovered. It was also intended to exploit the new coastal marker of the original blockships. The unknown element was the extent of German reaction, particularly as more destroyers were now available in Flanders to defend the coast. Keyes tried to insure against this by having 12 destroyers available to cover the raiders.

OPPOSITE
A German photograph taken after the raid and illustrating all three blockships. *Thetis* is at the top of this photo, with HMS *Iphigenia* central and HMS *Intrepid* bottom. The captains of the ships had followed Keyes' priorities in order to scuttle themselves at the canal entrance, rather than ram the lock gate. This was based on Keyes' briefing from exiled Belgian engineers, but he would later regret this, recognizing that damaging the lock gates would have caused more significant damage. The ships did not cause the channel to silt to the extent Keyes had expected and the Germans quickly opened a passage past them, removing jetties from the west side of the canal to enlarge the channel. [NHB]

Some of the raiders left behind on the Mole are marched into captivity. The 16 captured were predominantly Royal Marines who were unable to retreat to *Vindictive*, but four sailors were also captured from HMS *North Star*. [NHB]

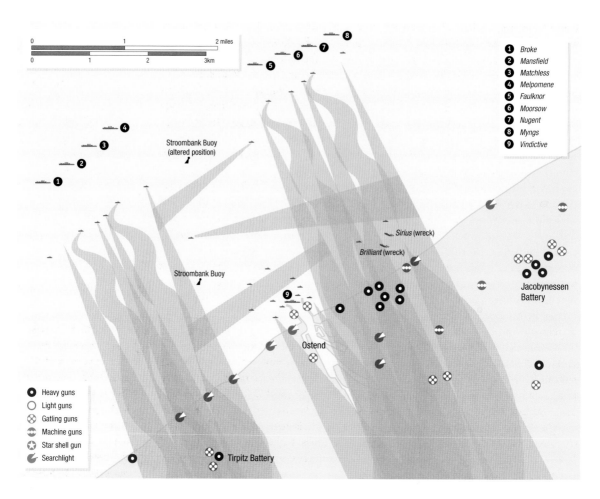

0   1   2 miles
0   1   2   3km

1 Broke
2 Mansfield
3 Matchless
4 Melpomene
5 Faulknor
6 Moorsow
7 Nugent
8 Myngs
9 Vindictive

Stroombank Buoy
(altered position)

Sirius (wreck)

Brilliant (wreck)

Jacobynessen
Battery

Stroombank Buoy

Ostend

○ Heavy guns
○ Light guns
⊗ Gatling guns
☺ Machine guns
☆ Star shell gun
✄ Searchlight

Tirpitz Battery

The second raid on Ostend, 9–20 May 1918. The grey areas on the map represent the smokescreens laid to cover the assault.

Vindictive and *Sappho* proceeded from Dunkirk but *Sappho*'s fitting out had only just been completed in time and on leaving Dunkirk she lost a joint in her boiler and was reduced to 6 knots. Cdre Lynes decided to leave her behind and attack with just *Vindictive*. By 0135hrs the task force was off Ostend and the water near them was being probed by a searchlight but there was no firing as the craft laid a smokescreen. Cdre Lynes ordered his force, including monitors, coastal guns and aircraft to open fire at 0143hrs. Within minutes a local fog had come down, sharply reducing visibility immediately around the task force, though the guns and 214 Sqn RAF continued their harassing bombardment throughout. At around the same time the task force had been detected by two German torpedo boats who signalled their presence. These boats then left the area to allow the coastal artillery free rein. By 0200hrs *Vindictive* was approaching the channel entrance, supported by small craft which were attacking the canal pierheads. Unable to observe their target the defenders laid down a maximum barrage across the entrance to the canal. While the poor visibility protected *Vindictive* it also worked against her finding the canal entrance and she was reduced to steaming parallel to the coast and then having the coastal forces light a million-candle-power flare close to the western pier of the entrance. While this would have been disastrous in most circumstances, in the poor light it provided just enough illumination for *Vindictive* to detect the entrance but inevitably intensified the fire on her. As she entered the canal her captain, Cdr Godsal, was killed and Lt Crutchley took command. However *Vindictive* was now aground on the eastern pier just on the edge of the shipping land. The plan had been to run her aground on the western pier and use the tide to swing her across the shipping. But the ship could not be re-floated and was therefore scuttled and, with what was now their almost customary skill and gallantry, the crews of ML 254 and ML 276 rescued the survivors of *Vindictive*. Some measure of the action can be estimated from the fact that ML 276 was hit in 55 places during the raid. By 0230hrs the raiders had withdrawn, with HMS *Warwick*, again functioning as Keyes' flagship, meeting ML 254 which was sinking from her damage. Her crew and 37 survivors from *Vindictive* were picked up but at 0400hrs *Warwick* struck a mine and was heavily damaged and was nursed back into Dover at 1630hrs, the last of the raiders to return.

Keyes was again well aware of the failure at Ostend, with *Vindictive* only on the edge of the shipping channel rather than blocking it. He therefore proposed a third raid in the window of 6–10 June utilizing *Sappho* but also HMS *Swiftsure*, a pre-dreadnought battleship now placed in reserve. Displacing over 11,000 tons compared to the 3,500–6,000 tons of the previous blockships, it was intended she should make a more significant obstacle. Her main armament was removed to reduce her draft but her 6in guns and her armour, proof against 6in guns, would remain. The plan was that *Swiftsure* would ram the western pier and be turned across the channel by the tide in the manner planned for *Vindictive*, with *Sappho* ramming her stern round to increase the effect.

Keyes selected Cdr Andrew Cunningham, an experienced destroyer commander and excellent ship handler, who would go on to fame as an admiral in World War II, to command *Swiftsure*. His crew were all volunteers from Chatham, many of whom had participated in the earlier raids, and the ship was fitted with anti-mine paravanes, as it was estimated that mines would almost certainly now have been laid off the canal entrance. The ships had completed full power trials at 18 knots but days before the operation it was cancelled on the orders of Weymss. Keyes was disappointed but later wrote, 'I hated giving it up, but at the same time really felt relieved, as I did not want to risk any more of my gallant people.'[25]

9–10 MAY 1918

Assault on Ostend.

HMS *Vindictive* aground against the eastern pier at the canal entrance at Ostend, following the raid of 10 May 1918. *Vindictive*'s final approach to the canal entrance was handicapped by the same poor visibility that allowed deep penetration of the defences. Her captain was killed at a critical moment and so the ship ran aground against the eastern, rather than the western pier. Against the western pier it was planned that the tide would swing the ship across the channel but in her actual position she did not block the channel. Visible on the deck are the remains of Sgt Finch's foretop, which was cut down by the Germans, as were the ship's funnels. This was done to reduce the ship's silhouette, which could have been a used as an aid in further bombardments. [NHB]

Engl. Kreuzer Vendictive nach dem Angriff auf Ostende.

---

25 Keyes, Sir Roger, *Naval Memoirs*, op. cit., p.339.

ANALYSIS

The concept of attacking the Flanders ports to deal with the German Navy 'at source' was undoubtedly a sound proposition and one entirely aligned with Britain's long-term concerns. The difficulties then came when trying to translate this into definite action. Ideas of a short and mobile war in 1914 led to the Royal Navy's deferring to the British Army's request that the ports be left operational in order to support the expected early advance back into Belgium. However, as Keyes was to comment, for this to work the army would have to also be assuming that the Germans would not sabotage the ports on their withdrawal, exactly as did happen in 1918. It is possible that the Admiralty also did not object too strenuously because of its professional and consistently held view that any amount of sabotage of a port was a temporary expedient and that only occupation of the port could determine its long-term use.

This view was consistent with the general support the Admiralty then gave to the long series of concepts and plans for an advance on the Entente's left flank, which would either reoccupy the ports or place them within range of medium or field artillery, as opposed to a small number of very long-range guns. This would then allow intense, as opposed to intermittent bombardments, which would be sufficient to render their facilities untenable. These plans were not fulfilled as Britain was very much the junior partner in land forces in the coalition with France and Britain's strategic priority was to maintain this coalition. This meant that Britain generally had to follow French priorities on the western front until at least 1917, which focused the fighting away from the coastal sector. By mid-1917 the situation had changed and one of the motivations for the third battle of Ypres was an advance on the Flanders ports. This led to the very serious preparations for a large-scale advance on the coast and the 'Great Landing'. However Haig only ever viewed these as feasible as part of a general advance and the 'trenchlock' of Passchendaele meant that these conditions were never close to being met.

The reason that the issue of the Flanders ports became a more compelling issue only in 1917 was that this was the year that the threat from those ports evolved from being largely one of potential danger to actual threat. The ports were always dangerous by nature of their location but limited by the small size of ships they could support. The German Navy developed them only slowly, with much of the effort going into the measures for their force protection, as opposed to their offensive capability. This partly reflected continuing priorities elsewhere, with Flanders often ranking third for resources after the High Seas Fleet and the Baltic theatre. Only post-Jutland did Flanders start to receive a significantly higher priority and even that was relative and intermittent. What did change from that point, though, was that the Flanders assets were now used more aggressively. Unrestricted submarine warfare from February 1917 was the most obvious example of this but the series of destroyer raids on the Channel defences in the winter of 1916–17 was also a major worry for the Admiralty. U-Boats could cause huge general disruption and slowly strangle Britain if not effectively countered. However, major destroyer sorties into the Channel, if sustained and supported, had the potential to cause a much faster and more critical disruption to the army's short but vital communications route to France, a route that required 14 million troop movements between 1914 and 1918. Particularly if combined with a successful German offensive ashore such attacks had the potential for fundamental strategic consequences.

By late 1917 the use of convoys had removed some of the urgency from the U-Boat issue but equally Passchendaele had demonstrated that major advances or

A group of 'Vindictives' on board the damaged ship following the raid. These men illustrate the wide range of uniform worn during the attack. Such images were also a significant element in the Royal Navy's campaign to emphasize the great gallantry of the raiders and the participation of sailors and marines from across the naval service. [RNM]

landings against the Flanders ports were not currently feasible. It was in this context of frustration that personality emerged as a key element in launching the raids, as much as any shift in the strategic situation. Jellicoe's and Bacon's positions on the new Channel barrages and raiding the Flanders ports were not radically different from those of Wemyss and Keyes, and preparation for both measures began under their command, but Wemyss and Keyes conveyed a more offensive optimistic attitude to dealing with the issues.

Keyes then drove on planning and preparation for the raids and without his leadership and determination it must be doubtful that they would ever have occurred. He is often seen as reckless and self-serving in his determination to persist, compromising his own pre-condition for a dark night. While there is undoubtedly a strong element of this in his motivation it must also be placed in context. Keyes saw the raids as part of a larger picture including his innovations with the Channel barrages and the requirement to defend army communications, both of which were potentially vulnerable to attack by surface ships from Flanders. The raid was designed as much against the operations of these destroyers as against the U-Boats. It was also designed against the morale and confidence of the German Navy in Flanders, meant to make them anxious about their own bases and their protection, rather than focused on taking offensive action into the Channel. The significance of this factor only increased during the planning of the raids due to the German offensive in France and the very real possibility that the land forces might have to retreat back behind Dunkirk in order to shorten their line, thus vastly improving the German Navy's physical position on the Flanders coast.

Keyes was also keen both to raise the morale of the Royal Navy internally and to improve its external reputation, two closely linked goals. This was one of the reasons for his determination to push ahead with offensive action if at all possible and why he deliberately structured his assault force to include all the elements of the naval service. It was also one of the reasons he was ruthless with risking his manpower, both in illuminating the Channel barrier and on the raids, as he constantly compared that risk with that which the army was taking ashore.

The original memorial to the raid, dedicated by King Albert of Belgium on 23 April 1942 in the presence of Keyes and many of the raiders. It portrayed St George slaying the dragon, but was destroyed by the Germans during their occupation of 1940–44. [NHB]

There have been numerous criticisms of the planning and preparation of Operation *Z.O.*, citing points such as the failure of the special parapet anchors to secure ships to the Mole and the fact that the training of the storming parties did not reflect recent experience. Keyes does, though, seem to have broadly done his best with the materials and time available, while preserving sufficient security and strongly motivating his personnel. Securing some personnel more experienced in recent land fighting for the landing parties was one of his ambitions and would undoubtedly have helped on the Mole, avoiding errors such as the clustering and resulting heavy casualties of the senior officers during *Vindictive*'s final approach. It would not, however, have altered the requirement for vigorous offensive action, with inevitably heavy casualties in order to create an effective diversion. Many innovative measures were successfully used, such as C.3's self-destruction and the extensive use of smokescreens, and the assault force penetrated a fully prepared defensive zone of nearly 25 miles to within just half a mile before they were discovered.

All these innovations, though, were dependent for their success on the incredible gallantry of the raiders. While the participants' bravery was never in doubt, the extent to which Keyes ensured they understood the intent behind their orders and were allowed to make judgements on the spot, what would today be called 'mission analysis', is more problematic. The main example of this came with HMS *Intrepid*'s clear run at the canal lock gate. It seems there was no reason why Lt Bonham-Carter could not have rammed his ship against the gate but he chose to sink it in the canal entrance, in strict accordance with his orders, even though HMS *Thetis* had now dropped out. It seems that though Keyes had provided multiple blockships in order to ensure redundancy, precisely because he thought it very likely that all the ships would not get through, the orders did not indicate priority targets or give the ship commanders any latitude. Keyes later wrote that his initial assessment that all the blockships should attack the lock was modified by consultations with Belgian engineers who stressed the silting effect of blockships at the entrance but that he ultimately came to regret following this advice.

In material terms the Royal Navy suffered no great losses. The blockships and C.3 were, by definition, expendable and the loss of *North Star* and three motor launches was not significant in the overall naval balance. The number of servicemen who became casualties in the raids on Zeebrugge and Ostend was, however, considerable. Keyes' despatch on Zeebrugge reported 176 killed, 412 wounded and 49 missing, a total of 637 casualties, while the German estimate of British losses was 214 killed, 383 wounded and 19 taken prisoner, a total of 616. A best final estimate of British dead includes those lost in CMB 33A and at the second attempt at Ostend, as remarkably there were no British deaths during the first attempt there. Including those who died of wounds up to the end of World War I the total is at least 240. By contrast German losses in both raids were only 11 dead and 24 wounded, a total of 35.

Nevertheless, losses during the operations were never going to be the main criterion against which the raids were judged. For both sides the principal impact was to be on future operations and perceptions. In terms of activity Keyes made great claims for success, despite the failure at Ostend and his strenuous efforts to address this. Though he admitted that smaller submarines and torpedo boats were soon able to exit Zeebrugge as well as Ostend, he cited aerial photographs that showed many larger submarines and destroyers alongside in Bruges until late June. On 23 May Wemyss told the War Cabinet that there were 24 destroyers and 12 submarines apparently 'locked' in Bruges. Keyes claimed that disruption continued beyond this but also criticized the new RAF for failing to follow up the raid with air attacks on the ships, submarines, ports and particularly the area near Zeebrugge lock where the Germans had removed two small wharfs in order to widen the channel around the blockships. Contrasting this with the pre-RAF command arrangements when he would have had his own RNAS squadrons under command he would later use the issue to campaign for the return of organic aircraft to the Royal Navy.

Publicly the German stance was that the raid did not affect naval operations even for a day and for the smaller submarines and torpedo boats this was true, with both types navigating past the blockships on 24–25 April, something that was immediately known to NID at the Admiralty via radio intercepts but which it was decided not to publicize. The Germans did, however, apply more caution to the passage of their larger submarine types and destroyers, vessels that also generally did not use Ostend because of its more restricted canal and because of the heavier shelling of the port. Only after dredging around the blockships did a large submarine use Zeebrugge on 4 May and a destroyer flotilla on the 14th. The early aerial photographs therefore do show effectively immobilized ships. The later ones can be explained either by the presence of ships that were simply inactive on the day in question or by the little-appreciated fact that the canal was blocked again after the raid. This was the culmination of all the other measures taken against the ports. On 28 May the lock gate was struck by an aerial bomb which closed the canal for a week. Then on 9 June the gate was hit again by a coastal bombardment. British sources thought that this put the lock out of action for about five days but German sources credit it with closing the canal until the end of June. Therefore the cumulative effect of the raid and the bombardments was that the canal was effectively closed for larger submarines and destroyers for 50 of the 70 days from 23 April.

By July when the canal again began regular operations the local defences had been further enhanced but the actual usage of the Flanders ports was in decline, with effective

A group of raiders at a reunion in 1963. The photograph is taken in Ostend in front of the bow section of HMS *Vindictive*, the section having been salvaged after the war to provide a memorial. [RNM]

submarine strength dropping from 24 in June to just 13 by September. This related strongly to the much increased dangers of the Channel barrages. In the first quarter of 1918 8 per cent of attempted submarine passages through the Channel had resulted in a loss; in the second quarter this had dropped to 33 per cent and by the third it was 40 per cent of a steadily declining sample as the route was simply classed as non-viable. Without that route the advantage of Flanders-based submarines compared to German based ones was nullified, especially if the Flanders bases were considered more vulnerable to disruption. This might indicate that Keyes' work on the Channel barrages was far more significant than his more dramatic programme of raids, but in Keyes' mind they were always seen as complementary. The one effective German counter to the increased danger of the Channel barrage was further destroyer raids from Flanders, supported if possible by heavier units from the High Seas Fleet, particularly if they wanted to push on and disrupt the army's communications. However the Germans, now conscious of the vulnerability of their forward bases to disruption and psychologically shocked that the Royal Navy had managed to penetrate to the very centre of a key defended zone, actually chose to edge back into the greater safety of German waters, increasingly ceding uncontested control of the previously contested Channel waters to the British. In October, almost exactly four years after they had arrived, the MarineKorps Flandern evacuated Ostend and Zeebrugge, wrecking the ports and locks as they left, as Keyes had predicted. On 24 October the German Navy issued plans for a full-scale naval sortie against the Thames Estuary and the now Entente-occupied Flanders coast, with the fleet covering a raiding force of destroyers and cruisers. The sortie never occurred because of the navy's widespread mutiny.

One of the German Navy's greatest frustrations following the raids, particularly given their minimal casualties and that at least their smaller vessels had continued to operate without major disruption, was, in the words of Admiral Jacobsen, the historian of the MarineKorps Flandern, that 'whopping great lies were rained down on the trusting English citizens and the rest of the German hating world'. Keyes had always intended that one effect would be to boost the morale of the Royal Navy and increase its reputation and he had written to Beatty before the raid, 'even if we don't achieve all we are setting out to do – we will accomplish a good deal for the credit of the Service, and we will give the enemy a bad night'. This was achieved and probably beyond all his expectations, with the effect magnified by the desperate war situation elsewhere; the *Daily Mail* was typical when it reported on 24 April, 'An Immortal Deed, Our High Command today believes in using our sea-power to strike and not merely to fend off blows.' Whatever the operational realities of the effects of the blockships, the raids undeniably indicated that the Royal Navy had penetrated into the heart of a German base and the heroism of the sailors and marines required no exaggeration. Capt William Fisher, Director of the Anti-Submarine Division of the Admiralty, wrote to Keyes, 'You have earned the gratitude of the whole Navy. We are vindicated. We can put up our heads again.'[26] The morale effect was also taken up over the wider Allies, with Marshal Foch writing of it as 'a superb manoeuvre involving a common spirit of supreme sacrifice' and Admiral Sims of the USN stating that, 'Few incidents of the Great War had a greater influence in inspiring enthusiasm in the fighting forces and increasing their morale than the successful attack upon Zeebrugge.'[27] Even allowing for Allied sympathies and wartime propaganda the raids did provide a genuine boost, the effect being increased by coming at a time of relentlessly bad news.

---

26 Halpern, Paul, *Naval History*, op. cit. pp.412 and 415.
27 Carpenter, Alfred, *The Blocking of Zeebrugge*, op. cit., pp.xi–xiv.

CONCLUSION

The Royal Navy played a key role in World War I. The blockade, when combined with Germany's attempts to sustain huge land campaigns, was a vital element of victory, with the Entente powers able to draw on the resources of the world while Germany was unable to do so. Major naval actions, though, were few and the lack of a decisive victory over the German fleet was frustrating, even when a hugely favourable strategic balance was being maintained. The Royal Navy was also frustrated by the relative success of Germany's raiding of commerce with submarines. Though effective counters were found these were more able to control the scale of the problem than to solve it and again led to much vital but often unrewarding escort, patrol and picket work for the sailors.

Such frustration was combined with an awareness of the scale of loss and effort that the land forces were having to bear, with the army suffering an average of 10,000 killed a month in 1918. This was also dramatically illustrated by the fact that the Royal Naval Division was never more than 5 per cent of the Royal Navy's strength but accounted for 40 per cent of its fatal casualties. It was in this context that a naval staff study could comment, when considering the 'Great Landing', that, 'At worst total failure involved the loss of six 12-inch monitors and one division of troops, a loss which, though regrettable, was not of vital importance.' In this situation Admiral Keyes was the driving force behind planning and mounting the Zeebrugge and Ostend raids, as part of a wider package of operational measures in the Channel. He was motivated by a compound of personal, operational and morale factors to ensure that the raids took place and he was both inspirational and ruthless with his manpower to achieve the offensive action he deemed essential in war. He also appreciated the balancing of his risks and losses compared to the wider war. In the context of that war, and his wider campaign, he achieved physical results which were less than he claimed but which still had some significance and psychological effects that were much greater. The raids on Zeebrugge and Ostend were worthwhile, not least for the morale of the country and its allies at a time of unremittingly bad news, and the morale and reputation of the Royal Navy would have been lower had they not been launched.

The current memorial to the Zeebrugge raiders, located at the base of the modern port's harbour wall. [Author]

FURTHER READING AND BIBLIOGRAPHY

In writing this book I have been fortunate in having access to the Admiralty Library and the archives of the Naval Historical Branch and would like to thank Miss Jenny Wraight (Admiralty Librarian) and Mrs Kate Brett (Curator of the Naval Historical Branch) for their invaluable assistance, particularly Mrs Brett's in translating German documents. From these sources a series of vital official documents are available which enhance our understanding of the raids. In particular there is an originally secret Naval Staff document, *Reports on the Zeebrugge and Ostend Operations 22–23 April 1918 & Ostend Operations 10 May 1918*, which includes more than 80 primary accounts of the raids. Also important is the *Naval Staff Monograph (Historical), Volume VI, The Dover Command: Volume I* (March 1922) and *The Report of Committee Appointed to Examine the German Defences on the Belgian Coast* (1919) which is a detailed and lavishly illustrated summary of the defences, including important German documents. Finally the Naval Staff History *British Mining Operations 1939–1945* (1973) is important. Despite its title the first 40 pages are a detailed history of British mining operations in World War I.

Abbatiello, John, *Anti-Submarine Warfare in World War I, British Naval Aviation & the Defeat of the U-Boats*, Routledge (London, 2006). Chapter 4 is the best summary of air operations against the Flanders ports.

Bacon, Sir Reginald, *The Concise Story of the Dover Patrol*, Hutchinson (London, 1932)

Black, Nicholas, *The British Naval Staff in the First World War*, Boydell Press (Woodbridge, 2009)

Carpenter, Alfred, *The Blocking of Zeebrugge*, Herbert Jenkins (London, 1925)

Cunningham, Viscount Andrew, *A Sailor's Odyssey*, Hutchinson (London, 1951)

The Mole extension today during a battlefield study by the crew of HMS *Albion*, with Commander Jim Lines RN in the foreground. A landing platform dock (LPD), HMS *Albion* is one of the Royal Navy's three major amphibious ships and a modern successor to HMS *Vindictive* but exploiting far more sophisticated capabilities. A modern assault ship will seek to 'stand off' its target to the greatest extent possible, deploying its raiders by helicopter, boat and specialized landing craft. [Author]

Dickinson, Harry, 'The Zeebrugge & Ostend Raids, Operation ZO, April 1918' in Lovering, Tristan, *Amphibious Assault, Manoeuvre from the Sea*, Seafarer (Woodbridge, 2007). The best short summary of the raids.

Grant, Roger, *U-Boat Intelligence 1914–1918*, Putnam (London, 1969)

Halpern, Paul, *The Keyes Papers, Volume I, 1914–1918*, Naval Records Society (London, 1972). An invaluable volume of documents, many of which deal with all aspects of the general naval situation and the raids.

Halpern, Paul, *A Naval History of World War I*, UCL Press (London, 1995). The best naval history of World War I.

Herwig, Holger, *Luxury Fleet, The Imperial German Navy 1888–1918*, George Allen & Unwin (London, 1980)

Jackson, John, *Private 12768, Memoir of a Tommy*, Tempus (Stroud, 2004)

Karau, Mark, 'Wielding the Dagger': The MarineKorps Flandern & The German War Effort, 1914–1918*, Praeger (London, 2003)

Karau, Mark, 'Twisting the Dragon's Tail: The Zeebrugge and Ostend Raids of 1918', *The Journal of Military History* Volume 67 (April 2003). Karau's book and article are the most important works in English on the German side of the raids and all elements of the German Navy's involvement in Flanders. It is unfortunate that they are not more widely known, seeming not to have been consulted in the new histories of the raids since 2003.

Kendall, Paul, *The Zeebrugge Raid 1918*, Spellmount (Stroud, 2008). A detailed history of the Zeebrugge Raid, particularly strong on personal accounts and the full stories of many of the British participants.

Keyes, Sir Roger, *The Naval Memoirs of Admiral of the Fleet Sir Roger Keyes, Volume II, Scapa Flow to the Dover Straits 1916–1918*, Thornton Butterworth, (London, 1935)

Keyes, Lord Roger, *Amphibious Warfare and Combined Operations*, Cambridge UP (Cambridge, 1943)

Kindell, Don, *Royal Navy Roll of Honour, World War I*, Naval-History.Net (Penarth, 2009). The best possible source for Royal Navy deaths in World War I. It is also available online as a searchable download at www.naval-history.net

Lake, Deborah, *The Zeebrugge and Ostend Raids 1918*, Leo Cooper (Barnsley, 2002)

Marder, Arthur, *From the Dreadnought to Scapa Flow, the Royal Navy in the Fisher Era, 1904–1919, Volume V, Victory & Aftermath* (January 1918 – June 1919), Oxford UP (London, 1970)

McGreal, Stephen, *Zeebrugge & Ostend Raids*, Pen & Sword, (Barnsley, 2007). Includes a valuable section on cemeteries, memorials and touring the battlefields today.

Newbolt, Henry, *Naval Operations, Volume V*, Longman (London, 1931)

Prior, Robin & Wilson, Trevor, *Command on the Western Front, The Military Career of Sir Henry Rawlinson 1914–1918*, Blackwell (London, 1992)

Prior, Robin & Wilson, Trevor, *Passchendaele, The Untold Story*, Yale University Press (London 2002). Provides the best exploration of the interaction between the issues of the Flanders bases and the third battle of Ypres.

Thompson, Julian, *The Royal Marines, From Sea Soldiers to a Special Force*, Sidgwick & Jackson (London, 2000)

Wiest, Andrew, *Passchendaele and the Royal Navy*, Greenwood Press (London, 1995)

Williamson, Gordon, *U-Boats of the Kaiser's Navy*, Osprey (Oxford, 2002)

Wright, Harry, *Memoirs of Sergeant Harry Wright (Zeebrugge & Aftermath)*, Royal Marines Historical Society (Portsmouth, 1990)

INDEX

References to illustrations are shown in **bold**.